Lover of the Wind, Flower

Jung-rok Lee

Legend Times

Published by Legend Times Group
51 Gower Street, London, WC1E 6HJ
info@legendtimesgroup.co.uk | www.legendpress.co.uk

Contents © Jung-rok Lee 2023

The right of the above author to be identified as the author of this work has been asserted in accordance with the Copyright, Designs and Patents Act 1988. British Library Cataloguing in Publication Data available.

First Edition

First published in Korean by Saemmoon Book Publishing in 2023 | www.saemmoon.co.kr

Translated by Lee, Sol
Figures by Joo Seung-in and others
Editorial design by Soon-ok Shin

Paperback ISBN: 9781918291964

[Saemmoon Collection]

\<Convergence Joint Poetry Selection>
Love was beautiful for its name
Aria, poetry flows in the birch forest
Poetry, read the star and tell the fortune
A broken wheel
The revolution dreamt by the first snow
The sound of an owl
That is how I love you(Han Yongun Collective Poetry)
Into the turquoise love
The shadow of the moon across the private gateway
An absurd poet in my family
The maid of the sun
A flower that adores the wind

\<Personal Poetry Collection>
Love I met on the trail (Lee Jeong-rok)
You bloom the flame inside me (Jang Joo-woo)
I'm happy to dream (In Jeong-hee)
Prince of the chestnut house (Park Gil-dong)
God's gift~Mother (Lee In-young)
Poetry paradise (Seo Chang-won)
The song of life God has granted me (Park Dong-hee)
I cried because I missed you (Kang Seong -hwa)
A thousand years of songs sung by the wind (Kim Yeong-woon)
I send a thousand yearnigs (Choi Seong-hak)
The reason I love flower (Lee Jeong-rok)
When love flowers bloom (Oh Hee-seok)
The love song of Taehwa river (Lee Soo-dal)
The road to find stars (Choi Jin-taek, Ko Yeong-hee)
The spring bandit (Seo Chang-won)
A tree where birds grow (Kim Hyun-mi)
The magic of the spring maiden (Lee Dong-chun)
One third of a humming (Mo Sang-cheol)
A longing that bloomed in the longing (Ko Yi-soon)
To the bird up high (Ko Wook-hyang)
I miss you, poem (Kim Dong-cheol)
The chair of the wind (Nam Mi-sook)

A woman dreaming of star flowers (Kim Choon-ja)
Give me a blue scent (Park Rae-seon)
It's so hard to love (Seo Chang-won)
Double-eyed Wolf (Lee Jeong rok)
From flower, to the wind (Lee Jeong-rok)
I miss you at the Auraji river (Lee Jong-sik)
A chorus of flowers (Lee Jeong-hye)
On my way back from the country house (Choi Jin-taek)
Love of beauty (Seo Chang-won)
The day when the moon loved the star (Jeong se-il)
Empire of the wind (Jeong Wan-sik)

{Lee Jeong-rok Personal Collection}

<Written by>
Love I met on the trail (1st Edition published 1993)
Double-eyed Wolf (2nd Editio)
-Displayed at Kyobo Bookstore Golden Zone
Love I met on the trail (2nd, 3rd, 4th, 5th Edition-2020)
-Displayed at Kyobo Book store Golden
From Flower to the Wind
Lover of the Wind, Flower

<Co-author>
Love was beautiful for its name
Aria, poetry flowers in the birch forest
Poetry, read the star and tell the fortune
A broken wheel
The revolution dreamt by the first snow
Into the turquoise love
The shadow of the moon across the private gateway
An absurd poet in my family
The maid of the Sun
A flower that adores the wind and 62 other volumes

<Convergence Joint Poetry Selection>
That is how I love you (Han Yongun Collective Poetry)

Lee Jeong-rok

Pen name : Saemteo
Art name : Seungmok, Jiyul
Suin, Jebek
Career : Poem, sijo, essay,
 novel, critique

Education
Seoul National University Department of Fashion and Textiles
Soongsil University Graduate School of Small Business MBA
Completed Korea University Creative Poetry Course
Professor of Daelim University, Leisure, Culture and Sports Course
Professor of Daelim University, Literature College
Head of Saemmoon Lifelong Education Center
Head of Saemmoon Lifelong Cyber Education Center

Career (Current)
Head of Book Publishing Saemmoon
Director of Literary Group Saemmoon
Director of the Saem Writers Association
Member of the Korean Writers Association
Chairman of PEN Korea Culture Information Committee
Director of Korea Modern Poets Association
Head of Han Yongun Literature
Head of Korean Literature
Director of Four Seasons Poetry Center
Head of Saemmoon Shopping Mall
Head of Steering Committee for Han Yongun Literature Award
Head of Steering Committee for Han Yongun National Recitation Award
Member of Korea Music Copyright Association (KOMCA)
Member of Korea Copyright Commission
Head of Saemmoon Song Association
Publisher of Saemmoon Poem Collection

Media
Publisher and head of Saemmoon News

Awards
1992 Debut as a poet
1993 Published first poetry collection(The love I met on the trail)
Grand Prize of Han Yongun Literature Award
Saemteo Literature Award, Korea Literature Award
Korea Story Literature Award,
Saemteo Literature Award(Sijo), Saemteo Literature Award(Essay)
Saemteo Literature Award(Critique), Saemteo Literature Award(Novel)
Accepted by International Oriental Painting Award(Tokyo Art Center, Japan)

Registration
Korean Biographical Encyclopedia (Leader of the Contemporary History
By National Citation and Awards Committee)
Artist Registration (Korea Artist Welfare Foundation)

Exhibition
National Korean Paiting (2017), Uijeongbu, Seoul Arts Center
International Oriental Painting (2017), Tokyo Art Center, Japan

Memorial Stone
Saemteo Poetry Park
(Misan-myeon, Boryeong-gun, South Chungcheong Province)

Sending purple scent to those who are weary

Literature is a language art, and poetry is at the core of it.

This art is not just spoken through words, but it comes from our hearts. Only when we spit out the true feeling in our hearts shall the language be of greatest beauty.

Beautiful language is not a common phenomenon. It only pours out from earnest longing. And this longing is born from desperate love. The spring of love must well up our bottomless abyss without ceasing.

Lover of the Wind, Flower is my sixth collection of poems to be published, and it came with a great deal of contemplation. Which work or which imagery should I approach my readers with? What kind of dream should I deliver to them? These were the subjects and prepositions that I long-pondered on.

Before this, my works mostly targeted the elderly. However, this sixth collection is filled with lyrical poems aimed at young readers in their teens, 20s, 30s, and 40s. With hope to communicate with them through works that could be read without much burden, I wrote, revised, and examined the lines with devotion.

'Let me carry a gift to my young friends, just as I write a letter to my lover, friend, and acquaintances. Rather than heavy or difficult poems, why not try lyrical poems with sparkling language of romance? I could fill my letter with romantic poems that would touch their sensitivities just like the speaking poems pursued by Rainer Maria Rilke and Robert Browning in the 18th to 19th Centuries.'

As the era of practical scientism arrived and developed at a fearful speed, materialism spread over almost everything. In reaction to high-tech media pouring out, human emotions are drying up, and extreme individualism prevails. Furthermore, the COVID-19 pandemic have led to extended social isolation. There are issues that let us down; unemployment, sexual inequality and conflict, income gap, raising children, nuclear family, family disintegration, aging society and burden of supporting elderlies, generation conflicts······ Amid these problems, it is not rare to find Millenials or Gen Zs fallen into loneliness, depression, distorted characters, and traumas.

So my challenge was how to send comfort and support to the younger generation, instill dreams and hopes in their souls, and heal their minds and bodies.

In this case, I tried my best to think outside the widespread emotions of the complicated 'postmodernism' poetry and encourage readers to recover their pure minds. My hope behind writing this book has been to smear into the readers' souls with works that can talk to them like pictures and poems.

For 40 years of my life, I have lived as a poet and businessman at the same time, unable to make ends meet only through writing. I have run all kinds of businesses; manufacture, chemistry, language materials, trade, and R&D for distribution. I have created jobs for around 20,000 employees, and received at least 300 or more patents including invention patent, utility model, design, and trademark registration. Then I dreamed of new technology development companies, venture companies, ISO14001, ISO19001, standardized certification companies, and registering for KOSDAQ. 20 years I spent, operating a local investment company in China. Once, the IMF and real-name financial system struck and left me in agony. Then, I half died as a vegetable after a highway vehicle collision. 17 days later when I woke up in the intensive care unit, I finally had the chance to look back at myself and saw that I had been a monster, not a man. Not a poet, either. I wailed and wept for the whole three months and fifteen days at that cold, suffocating hospital bed.

From that point, I started emptying out everything within myself. The evil, corrupt, humiliation, sorrow and pain all poured out from my soul. Then I had the room to recall my original purity and fill the soul up again.

I went out to search again for the pure emotion that I had been born with. I was truly born again.

I started my literary career in 1992 and published my first collection of poems, *Love I Met on the Walkway*, in 1993. Yet the crisis in my business disabled any sort of publication ceremony or sharing the news with my family and friends.

The reason is that the atmosphere of the time was harsh on poetry. The public would criticize and jeer at me that I had wasted time on talking romance and bragging when I could have contributed to the country's industrialization and economic development by working, running a business, paying employees' salaries, and feeding my family. Those were the days. Plus, born as the son of a poor farmer and craftsman, I had suffered a lot from a young age. The mission to overcome my fate, succeed, and raise my family always came first.

Therefore, I had to postpone writing in full-swing and continue on with my business while writing occasionally. But when I counted the works 40 years later, I was surprised to find about 15,000 poems, sijo[1], essays, and column manuscripts piled up in the dust.

In 1993, the first collection of poetry, *Love I Met on the Walkway* was re-published by *Saemmoon Sight* and selected as the best-seller by Kyobo Bookstore. It received the honor of being displayed at the Golden Zone, the Gwanghwamun exhibition section of Kyobo Bookstore.

---

1) Korean traditional three-stanza poem

4

Since then, I have published a series of collections, *The Reason I Love Flowers*, *Both-eyed Wolf*, and *Flower to the Wind* in *Saemmoon Sight*, recording best-sellers and successively making their way into the Golden Zone of Kyobo Bookstore.

Now, let's take some time to ask myself questions. What is meta-cognition or super-cognition?

To jump to the conclusion, it is 'knowing what I know and what I mistake for knowing.'

Then why does a poet write poems?

What made him or her become a poet?

I think this 'why' question helped me a lot to learn 'what I mistake for knowing'.

In philosophy, the question 'why' leads to finding the source of the problem.

That is, asking the meaning and reason of existence is actually a poet's self-censorship process to become a dignified human being. In addition, 'why' suggests the direction to answer 'what' and 'how.'

It can be said that I was motivated to write a poem because of the desire to express myself. I enjoyed finding meaning and value by recording the feelings I saw, heard, and felt. It was when I realized myself expressing my feelings in a poetic manner that I became a poet.

My time is the branches tightly intertwined with the flower trees. A branch opens its arms gently, enduring everything until it blooms.

The tree breaks with pain, shedding tears using all its strength. It raises its flower stand to bloom, and the mournful buds shake in the wind.

It tries its best to open up a painful bud.

A flower tree is the mother of flowers. It is the mother's womb that makes ribs, backbones, imageries, fragrant longing and compassion, and bear the fruit of love.

Flowers bloom at the mother's joints.

Some flowers present fresh pheromone scents and songs. True, they have sophisticated and refreshing colors. But above all, they tell where love lies by releasing its scent.

The flower ticks the alarm clock that signals where my time hides, then spreads its wings wide. It runs toward me standing and waiting at the climax. And I hold my lover, the flower, and smell the scent.

I will rework this perfume and fill with it the hearts of my beloved readers.

May 10, 2022

Under the shade of flowers,
From Lee Jung-rok, Saemteo

A purple love song floating in the wind

- Son Hae-il

(Poet, Literary Critic, Professor, 35th President of International PEN Korea Headquarters)

It is said that Poet Lee Jung-rok will compile the sixth collection of his poems, *Lover of the Wind, Flower*. As we know, Lee Jung-rok has published several books of poetry as a leading poet with various social experiences. While serving as the chairman of the literary group Saemmoon, he operates a total of nine organizations under the group, including two educational institutions, a media company, publishing agency, four literary companies, private certification agency, and open market shopping mall. He is also a professor at a prestigious university, and his four poetry collections have become best-sellers, proceeding to *Golden Zone*, the only poetry corner of the Gwanghwamun exhibition hall of Kyobo Bookstore. He has surely been creating a fresh wind in the existing literary circles. He founded Saemteo Literature many years ago and developed it into an online and offline literary organization of 80,000 members. So far, he has published 11 volumes of Convergence Emotional Poetry, the first fusion collection of works by amateur writers, together with best established writers. The publisher *Saemmoon Sight* has become a best-selling brand giving birth to many best-selling poets. It also operates courses in department of poetry creation and poetry recitation, issues private certificates, and publishes online newspaper *Saemmoon News*.

In 2021, Saemteo established and held the first Han Yong-un Literature Award and Han Yong-un National Poetry Recitation Contest. It was supported by Jungnang-gu, Seoul, under the name of K-Literature Festival. As such, this poet is laying the foundation for the globalization of Korean literature by actively utilizing Korea's cutting-edge mass media functions and adding business mind to the pure literary works.

Today, Korea has stepped up as one of the world's top 10 economic powers. It is an IT powerhouse with innovative culture, economy, defense, and science. Moreover, K-POP, K-drama, Hanbok, and Korean food are leading the global culture. Our country, helplessly pushed back by the lack of weapons or tanks during the Korean War in 1950, has grown into a model country that has overcome the devastation of the war and achieved democracy and economic growth in a short period of time. It is encouraging to see this country as the world's sixth-largest military power in defense, building and exporting the world's strongest K9 self-propelled guns, K2 tanks, KF21 fighter jets, and combat ships, as well as semiconductor technology, automobiles, nuclear power, and ships.

In line with the change in Korea's international status, shouldn't Korean literature also expand its translation business and set up K-Literature that will lead the global literature? Shouldn't we honor Hangul, the world's most sophisticated writing system, and try to communicate with readers around the world with texts created using Hangul? It was in this context that I founded the PEN Translation Institute as the 35th chairman of the International PEN Korean Headquarters and held four world Korean writing contests, receiving 500 million won of subsidy every year.

Let us go back to Poet Lee Jung-rok's poetry collection. This is a collection of lyric poems for young readers in their teens, 20s, 30s, and 40s. Most of the works are emotional works that are read without much burden. They are written in the form of a letter and confession of love to your long-cherished lover or an unspecified number of readers. These poems are rather love letters with sparkling sense of language than heavy, complicated poetry. They are easily read, as they resemble the style of Western romantic poetry as well as Korea's Kim So-wol, Yoon Dong-ju, Baekseok, and Kim Young-rang. Instead of introducing individual works, I would like to sing this collection as "a purple love song floating in the wind."

In general, Korean poetry can be divided into the genres of "talking poetry" and "show poetry." And this collection of poems corresponds to the "talking poetry." Speaking poems are romantic love poems that stimulate the emotions of readers. They come from Rainer Maria Lilke and Browning in the 18th and 19th century Western world. On the other hand, Show poetry is influenced by modernism. It would not explain the concept in words, but portray a picture with literary devices such as metaphors, symbols, emphasis, and implications. As today's society develops and high-tech media emerges, human emotions are prone to dry up, with extreme individualism prevailing. People feel lonely, keep rough hearts, and practical scientism permeates our lives.

Literature is a mirror of the times. Some poems reflect the high-tech civilization and complex times, while we cannot overlook the reason behind Kim So-wol, Yoon Dong-ju, and Kim Young-rang being consistently cherished by general readers as a response to the difficult modern poetry. It is the reader's taste that a school varies widely regardless of right or wrong. It is up to the poet or writer to produce and supply various works so that readers can choose what to feed on according to their tastes. Looking back, I recall that my early works, *Sesame Flower* and *Dalmaji Flower* were loved as popular 'Bookrest Poems' by students at the time. And that popularity led me here. Those poems were easily and sentimentally read, having excellent compressibility, connotation, metaphorical imaging, and rhythm. They were poems of unexpected beauty.

Poet Lee Jung-rok's works have high quality, dignity, and completeness. And thus adding too many words to it would be totally unnecessary. Instead, I would like to convey only the overall impression to the readers. It is clear that this collection of poems will be loved by readers. I am simply lucky to get a glimpse of the best work that shakes my mind before the readers. I felt a real thrill after reading this. I truly wish it would receive great love from the readers, and I conclude this article with sincere congratulation on Poet Lee's publishing sixth collection of poems.

Pink-tinted sentiments to the fatigued

- Kim So-yeop

(Poet, Chair Professor at Daejeon University, President of the Korean Christian Culture and Arts Association)

Poet Lee Jung-rok is a middle-aged poet who has already published five books of poetry and received the honor of making it a best seller each time he published a new collection. I sincerely congratulate him on publishing his sixth collection of poems, *Lover of the Wind, Flower.*

These days, I am not sure if poetry has left us due to its complexity or if we have abandoned it, but it is undeniable that poems have gone more distant from the public since the arrival of their new alter ego, smartphones. That is what makes Poet Lee Jung-rok's publication more meaningful, as he has consistently written poems and pioneered the popularization and civilization of poetry amid this difficult reality.

Poems can be divided into two main trends. One is a poem that is easily read, and the other is a difficult poem that you can't grasp the feeling at once. General public prefer easy-to-read poems to hard-read poems that require brainwork. Regardless of how powerfully postmodernism dominates our society and lifestyles, a majority of readers goes for Kim So-wol's poetry based on emotions and lyricism. Even though the ambiguous and diverse lifestyles of the post-modern society have already swept through the world of poetry like a storm, ordinary readers would still choose to read easy, lyrical poems. In that respect, poet Lee Jung-rok is a poet with a large readership. No matter how good a poem is, what's the benefit if no one reads it?

Poet Lee Jung-rok is also the chairman of "Saemmoon" corporation, operating a total of nine companies including Saemmoon News, Saemmoon Sight Publishing, three literature groups; Saemmoon Literature, Han Yong-un Literature, and Korean Literature, a private certification agency, and an open-market Saemmoon shopping mall, etc. Altogether, he is running nine companies that are approved by the Korean government, registered as non-profit organizations by the Seoul city, and approved by Ministry of Strategy and Finance to issue donation receipts. As a representative of the prestigious Saemmoon Group, Lee Jung-rok has taken innovative approaches to utilize the characteristics of each groups; literature agencies, newspaper agencies, two education organizations, fostering talents in poetry and recitation, approved by the Ministry of Education, along with the selfishness of modern civilization. Thanks to Lee, literature has been planted into a whole, organic business system.

Recommendation Speech

As a result, it has formed a readership of 100,000 people, and many poetry books published in Saemmoon are becoming best-selling books. This is a milestone at a time when smartphone is taking away the reading population. It is truly a hope to find a new breakthrough for literature.

Lee Jung-rok works with lively sensitivity which he pours into writing and teaching poetry. This sixth collection of poems reflects his interpretation of love, radiantly sparkling as the sunlight. Think back to the emotions of your first love. The thrill, youth, and scent of spring! The pink color of love hangs over all of Lee's poems which I give credit to. Now is the time of absence of love. That is probably why young people overuse the term 'love.' This love is the life that gets us through. It is the foundation that adds color to our lives.

Poetry is the various shapes of love. And God is love. Unlike other species, God created humans in the form of Himself. In other words, humans resemble God's amazing creativity. That is how we got the talent to invent new things. Then, humans found love in God's creations; the Sun, Moon, stars, mountains, rivers, wind, flowers, trees, and people. They soon started expressing that love through language, which became poetry. Therefore, only by loving the nature, people, and the creator of all things, we can live a fulfilling and sincere life. Shelley, a poet that represents British romanticism, saw through that poetry is the pursuit of truth, goodness, and beauty. That is, a poet can only write poems of beauty and true emotions when he or she has lives a sincere life.

And here, Poet Lee Jung-rok wrote his poems upon this very sensitivity of love, singing the wind's fondness of flowers. The emotion of love flowing through the entire collection is ecstatically beautiful.

Perhaps, the readers of this collection will be unknowingly imbued with the pink-tinted love, spreading over his or her dried emotions. In this time of the history when everyone is exhausted and struggling due to the COVID-19 pandemic, I recommend that you take part in reading this collection of poems. I hope that our society will become more beautiful through sharing this collection of poems with your neighbors. For my last word, I sincerely congratulate the publication of Lee Jung-rok's 6th album, *Lover of the Wind, Flower*, and pray for the greatest blessings on his future literary works.

Lover of the Wind, **Flower**

K-poetry

Jung-rok Lee

Perhaps
The flowers
That bloom in pain
Might
Sooth
Your
Sadness
<Son of the wind, full quote>

Let your smile bloom
Today just like yesterday
With the most
Beautiful flower
With a Dazzling light
Let myself Bloom
<Smile, full quote>

Where have you been?
I was searching for you
Afraid that you wouldn't find me
I planted myself there
I'll rise in the morning
In your heart
<Morning star, full quote>

You
When you hide
Your existence
Leave me
In sorrow
Boo Hoo
<Love 2, full quote>

Contents

PART 1

The Naughty Secret of Flowers

Lilac

See your pretty purple crown
Prettier than those who envy you
More than diamond bluebells, than autumn bellflowers
Your color is incomparable

Looking for your purple scent
The day when I went on a spring walk
In that dewy mountain
I felt dizzy and hugged you

In the garden next to the jangdokdae[2]
I set up a honeymoon room with you
Made eye contact every day and night
I was drunk on the smell of your pure skin

Your violet-colored Hanbok[3]
As if propping up the taste inside the jangdokdae
And blessing our union
A fragrant day began

At your purple pride
Jealous birds made a fuss
The spring water was noisy
And April was crazy

---

2) Korean traditional earthenware where ancestors kept fermented kimchi or soybean products
3) Korean traditional costume

Missing Lila Flowers

Every year when April returns
My heart shivers and swells

Singing Besame Mucho
"Oh scent of lila flowers, give me a kiss"
The lila flowers
The purple scent of lilac
Make my heart tremble

The scent that smears deeper than the kiss
of your first love
Melts the frozen land of the earth
The burning passion

Elliot's
"April is the cruelest month,
breeding lilacs out of the dead land ..... "

Once in April, the street was filled with those
burning their youth with a cheerful rhythm
April, a purple month of love

In the green garden of April
I filled my hunger with purple dreams
and scents
Soothing my sadness
Those harsh days

Now it's merely a vague image
But you remain as a kind scent
The face I miss

Purple petals fall down
Memories clinging to each node
Deep longing
The scent of lila flowers fluttering in the
wind
Oh, the purple love

The Naughty Secret of Flowers

Half the day is dark, half the day is white
And know why

The dark half
is when we tint the flowers
with their naughty secret

The white half
is when we show off to a Casanova
the secret of flowers

The day Prince Casanova comes
Riding a white horse
to confess his love for me

I would bloom
to deliver the letter
of deep, beautiful secrets

Letters written in your language
are lost in the dark, spring dreams
And when you're lost in the maze

I will comfort you
I am the secret coordinate
to bring you out of mazes

Lover of the Wind, Flower 1

Perhaps
A casanova

Might
Steal
Your
Heart

Lover of the Wind, Flower 2

Your lips
Pale
And trembling

Perhaps The
Wind Might
Caress you

You are a Poem and I am a Flower

Look, you and I are very ill
I feel like I am you
And you are me
We've come through the rough times
As dearest friends

Throwing you into the wilderness
I have bloomed and fallen all life long
And how painful it must have been!
You were a black rock
And now you scatter as sand

All your life you've caressed
And cherished this world
This arrogant, heartless world
Now hacking
And abandoning you

Let's not be sad
The hard times we spent together
You and I will become sand and be scattered
When our sick souls are sown in the field
In the night sky
Will bloom the stars

Son of the wind

Perhaps
The flowers
That bloom in pain

Might
Sooth
Your
Sadness

Poet and Poem

Though a poet
Dies and
Disappears

His
Alter ego
Would not die
But live forever

His
Alter ego
Summons him

He
Is resurrected and
They forever
Live together

The reader
Holds them in the heart
Gains comfort
And heals the pain

With much love
And happiness

Flower

Perhaps
That wind

Might
Take away

Your
Sadness

The Red Dress

Hey you, shining Sun
Do you see my dress shining?
Since you're there during the day
Like you
I was able to shine

Hey you, shining star
See my dress glittering?
Since you're there at night
Like you
I was able to shine

Hey you, beautiful wild flower
See my dress glowing with beauty?
Since you're there blooming in pain
Like you
I was able to bloom

Hey you, floating cloud
See my dress light as feather?
Since you're there suffering and floating
Like you
I was able to be light

Do you hear the radiant, pure days?
The portrait of young days
The youth

The tearfully green days
The shining Sun and stars
Winds and clouds
A feast of beautiful flowers

Did you see the fierce, hot days?
The portrait of young days
My youth

Sunlight

Why do I walk with my eyes to the ground?
The worries of the world
Will not be the only reason

Head down, I couldn't see the world
So sometimes I looked up the sky
Until one day I took in your glare
Then I kept looking at you, devouring you

The more I indulge, the more cunning you become
I was dazzled by your beauty
But it's when you're in my heart
You shine brighter still
Did you know?
That secret fact
That thrilling fact

Flower Secret

When you wake up in the morning
Think about
How to please and delight people

The bright sunshine is for everyone
It gives us warmth
Fragrant flowers are for everyone
The give us fresh smile
And bright face is for everyone
It gives us friendliness

If you want to live a happy life
Erase your frown and rigid look
It has to be a smiley face

A gentle and cheerful life
Keeps your body and spirit healthy
And blooms the laughter of your family and neighbors

The flower of laughter
Is a better medicine than wild ginseng

This is the secret
Of blooming flowers

The Language of Tears

Your
Hot tears

Soak
My dry chest

And
My weary soul

It's the language of tears
And confession

The Love Song of Diamond Bluebell

1

You, wet with dew, are colored by the sun
Rainbow flowers bloom in the sky
Foggy flowers bloom in the pond

Angels sing from thousands of years apart
As if we hear it, we hear it
Your sad song sounds sweet

Love, love, love
Because you're there, because I'm here
It's our beautiful love

Your bright wait
It's my resting place
My eternal resting place

2

You, wet with sunlight, are colored
by the dew
The song of birds bloom among the
trees
The rustle of wind blooms in the
stream

The footsteps of gods thousands of
years apart
As if we hear it, we hear it
Your prelude sounds mysterious

Love, love, love
Because you're there, because I'm
here
It's our radiant love

Your purple fireworks
Are my living soul
My eternal living soul

Smile

Let your smile bloom
Today just like yesterday

With the most
Beautiful flower

With a
Dazzling light

Let myself
Bloom

Busan Love Song

With the kiss of sweetbrier by the Haeundae Beach
The sea turns bright red
And the burning kiss of Dongbaek Island Dulle-gil
Turns Camellia flowers bright red

Seagulls embroider the indigo sky with love signs
The silver sea sets afloat the buoy of love

A seabird's two feet trot along
Floating into the sea
Floating into the sea

Drumming waves, oh my love
Drumming waves, oh my love

The enchanting night with Yongdu mountain speciosa
Delivers scarlet light of dawn
With the delightful moonlight's confession over Yongkung bridge
One by one, my soul loosens up

Seabirds trot on a brass sunset, embroidering the star flower
The calm sea floats, blooming the moon flower

A seabird's two feet trot along
Floating into the sea
Floating into the sea

Drumming waves, oh my love
Drumming waves, oh my love

Passionate love

Over there
On top of that star
I'll be standing

So I can show
You
How much
I love you

The Prayer of Daffodils

A reply carried by the wind
Daffodil with wobbly eyes
Misty rain pouring down on her white chest

Lake filled with starlight and moonlight
The water shakes as the flower stand sobs
The trembling river bank collapses at last
And the history of flowers is swept away by the rough rapids

She gets wet by the rough spray
With wobbly eyes and a broken heart
Writes back a letter

Now my pistil cannot grasp your hands
I am leaving your side
Be happy, my dear

Faithful love

Always
I'll be standing here

So you
During your tiring walk
Can see me here

You
I love you

Spring Summoning

Pretty flowers bloom all at once
In the garden they bloom with pain
A longed-for face beams with smile

Answering with my two eyes
I reach out my hands to hold yours
One spring day when our love faded
Flowers poured down like a rain

The legend of my love for you ended
And came endless nights of pain
The rain of flowers fell

The moonlight moistened my heart
Starlight poured on me
Deeply embedding
Into my pale, naked heart
Shake it off, Shake it all off
Wetting my heart the star flower bloomed

The rainbow erased
Broken Ojakgyo[4]
The bridge of hatred and loathing
At every shattered piece of the bridge
I sit down to reflect

At last when everything is forgiven
Holding the past in my heart
One fragrant afternoon on a spring day
You bloom with smile in that flower garden

---

4) Refers to the bridge in a Korean traditional folk-tale. It is made by birds once a year to connect two longing lovers

Warmheartedness

In the bone-splitting
cold of winter

Precious things
leave
our sides

When spring comes
Will they come back?

Spring Breeze

Golden sunset heats up the mountain and fields
You embrace the cold earth with your burning heart

The wild grass sprouts green shoots
From every joint of leafless branches
It will soon burst into bloom

The spirit of the oxidized sunset
Lights up fire in the middle of the sky

Like the Gordian knot, with a single stroke
Stars are released from hibernation
Glittering like a star newborn by the black hole

What is it that calls in the bamboo forest
Where you stroll along?
Is it an owl, or the northern wind envying you?

Marriage

Passionately
love
someone

Live forever
and make a family

The only way
to live a decent life

Heartless Love

Though I hug and welcome the waist of our past
Why did you secretly
leave me behind?
I squeeze your unforgettable face into the thread of tears

The silent moonlight pouring over the bamboo forest
I have cut it into cloth
And made your clothes, picturing your figure in mind
I've picked the stars welled up in every dew
And set them along your dress

A pitch-dark night at the end of the moon
The longing for you flowing through the clouds
I will, too, secretly go and leave
But you are far away, faint in the sky
The water's deep, and I wanter through the swamp of grass

A White Magnolia

You grieve
And cry
My heart aches because of you

I know it hurts
But don't cry. Wait for me
I'll always be with you

Now
On the cuff
Of your pink sleeve

I am embroidering
you

You are Neomsabyeok

Met you at the Beojeong,
Geumsappa!
(Met you at the bus stop,
I fell in love right away.)

Solkkamal, I lost my jeongjul
You, Seureungheundeu!
(Frankly speaking, I lost my mind.
You, my dear, I love you.)

Kingwangjjang
You, Seureungheundeu!
(You are the best of best!
And I love you.)

Climbing over your Neomsabyeok,
DDD
(Trying to climb over your uncrossable wall,
my heart trembles.)

FR! Bbae-bak can't!
I send my heart by Beotaek
(For Real! Can't withdraw now!
I send my heart by Bus-delivery service.)

I'm not Deutbojap or Byeongmat
Please accept my love
(I'm not an anonymous jerk.
Please accept my love.)

You, Seureungheundeu!
(I love you!)

※※※
Neomsabyeok : An uncrossable wall
Beojeong : Bus stop
Geumsappa : Fall in love at first sight
Solkkamal : Frankly speaking
Lose Jeongjul : Lose my mind
Seureungheundeu : I love you
Kingwangjjang: Best of best
DDD: Shaking and trembling
FR: For real
Bbae-bak can't: Can't withdraw
Beotaek: Bus delivery service
Deutbojap: An anonymous man
Byeongmat: Unlikable jerk

PART 2

A Lifelong Letter

Let it Be Love

Let it be love with passion
The wild flowers in the field
With the excitement of greeting bees and butterflies
Bursting its buds with passion

Let it be love of purity
At dawn, sparrows move briskly
Washing their wings in bamboo tree water
Awakening their spirits

Let it be love of blessings
When thunder and lightning awaken the world
Rain and wind moisten the land
Together with colorful double rainbow

Let it be love of abundance
Golden waves in the field
Scarecrow singing a melody of the year
Dancing with richness

Let us be more gracious to one another
No matter how hard life is
And keep dreaming to live
Let it be love

Morning Star

Where have you been?
I was searching for you

Afraid that you wouldn't find me
I planted myself there

It'll rise in the morning
In your heart

The Value of Love

Although
You may be
Not so great at all

Although
You, with nothing special,
Confess your love for me

I
To you
I'll bet my life
It's worth it

Your Universe
Is bright and clear

My
Thin, thin heart
Because of you I can breathe

My
Ragged, wounded heart
Finds cure in you

Love 1

You
When you reveal
Your existence

Are the
Most beautiful

Love 2

You
When you hide
Your existence

Leave me
In sorrow

Boo Hoo

Spring

Spring
Comes from the Ice Age
Comes from the frozen ground
Comes from the Antarctic seal's lifeline

Look at the Siberian birch
Peeling its body white with a fierce snowstorm
When spring comes,
the bare skin nourishes its forest family
to feed on and sprout new shoots

Love, without sacrificing its flesh,
Is not true love
Heart, without embracing one's pain
Is a cold, worn-off heart

Look at yourself now
Look back on who I am now

Life is born
From the passionate womb of hulled barley
Through the pain of a woman's life and death
By the blood-red cry of a cuckoo bird

Proposal

Your
Blue sound

Hanging Wind
Over the Moonlight
Played
Like a moonlight sonata

I love you

Waiting

- The First Snow Falls Like an Overture

That day
On that time
The first snow
Came like the L'Orfeo

There
At that cafe
In the mug waiting for him
The first white snow
Was lonely like the Lucio Silla

Then
In that winter
White tears
Poured like the poems of Jeitteles

Camellia Flower

You came and left
In the moonlight

You whispered
With the starlight sitting by the river

It was you
Came across the light of the stream
And gave me that tinted letter

How hot my heart was!
Should the water turn blood-red

How many times
Did I repeat the word of love!

My heart
Was enough to burn

April's Flower Letter

If I can't hear it for real
Even in my dreams
I will hear your voice

Like the sound of rain
Or the sound of wind
Even if it merely swirls around
I still hope to hear your voice

Was there a day I did not dream of you?
Was there a day I did not hold you in my arms?
Under the shade of red plum blossoms
I read your flower letter

A Lifelong Letter

Honey
It's a seedling of a star flower
Take it

Plant
This seedling
On your chest

When white
Moonlight
Pours down on it
My heart will bloom

It's then
When you will read my letter

Poetry

He will be reborn
The seeds he has sown
Sleeping in the dark
When the moist spring rain falls,
Will burst out poppy-pop-pop
And sprout their tender buds

He will open up the dark world and reincarnate
Then, in the hearts of the corrupt and evil
And the hearts of the weak and sick
He will infiltrate, root down
And spread the spore
That is beyond measure
He will fly them to their Universe

He will break through the corrupt and evil flesh
And through the weak and poor
The seeds will grow and grow
Blooming good and kind flowers
Bearing abundant good fruits
And because of his scent
The world will be bright, clear, and fragrant

Confession

The reason
I empty my heart
And give to you
The truth
Hidden in it

Is to hold
The sound
Of your soul
In it

Spring Sprout

Your
Voice
Is the sound of strong action
After a long hibernation

As I stand
In the dry air
Listening to the wind that passes by
I hear the blue sound

Huffing and puffing
Your voice is walking towards me

As I stand
In the dry air
Listening to the bare land
I hear the blue sound

Pushing up with a grunt
Your voice

Edelweiss

You are the Himalayan angel
White and pure

Singing love
You dream in the snow
and bloom

You guard the summit
The heaven

Today, again
We're in full bloom, aren't we?

We have bloomed
The snow flower blessing our
tomorrow

Angel of dreams and hope
You!

Scenery of the First Snow Day

Snow has many faces during winter
The thin strings of snow
Turns to heavy snowflakes like cotton fluff
Then it hails and flutters

An umbrella would be cumbersome
So I walk in the snow
The traffic of the city
Melted away all the snow
But the trees along the road are covered white
Getting sound asleep

In the distance, the bluish mountains
Are shouting out white flakes of snow
And the Avecs wearing long padded coats
Arm in arm, are filled with joy

The masks are blocking the world
But also the coldness of the wind
Have we gotten used to it?
We're filled again with bits of happiness

Snowflakes land on my glasses
Scolding with anger, to watch out and be careful
While city is indifferent and warm
The dusk is crawling

Destiny

You are
Even if you don't say it
Even if I don't have to wait

Before I notice
Come to me
Into my warm embrace

You want
My teary eyes
And burning lips

As if you've gotten used to it
from the star we lived before

Brava!

Love of Wind-plum Flowers

You're a flower
I'm the wind

Without the wind,
Flowers cannot shake or bloom
Without the wind,
Flowers cannot bear a baby

Without flowers,
The wind has no reason to live
The world without flowers
Has no love for the wind

When the wind approaches the flower
Flowers tremble
And with the shaking cross-wind
The heart of the wind trembles along

That is when the heart of flowers sway
Fluttering the incense of passion
Flowers bear life and give birth to babies

You're a flower
I'm the wind

Plum Blossoms in the Snow

In the snow
When you bloom the cold, cold bud

Camellia
Awakes from its sleep
And puts up a cherry light

The spring breeze
Drunk by your scent
Starts to blow

My Dear Red Plum Blossom

In her mournful bloom
My heart and soul shake

Her fragrant scent
Flood into my abyss

The morning when Dew struggling with heartache
Falls on the ground

The birds nod
And say good bye

But my forever friend
She raises the flower stalk and smile broadly

Dampening with her big smile
The gnarled wounds
Gain pink flesh again

Apricot Flower

Full of morning dew
An angel bloomed in solitude

For whom is this love song written?
It is a song for you
Who follows after the spring breeze?

Her charming shoulder dance
The angel's cruel and rare fragrance
Takes away the breath of a traveler

Embroider the white skirt hem
The bold pink dance greeting its lover
Joyfully and merrily dancing

Shy to see the lover's face
Turning slightly away
The figure makes me dizzy
Carrying a load of flowers
Walking and turning around
The traveler's heart pounding

Climbing up the dewy stem
Softly and joyfully, merrily
as it can be
What a heavenly dancer,
the apricot angel!

Spring Snow

Of course
She is
Never so easy

Into the chest of a spring lady
Blew a breathful of spring breeze
And now look at her so grumpy again
Burying everything white

Remember the last Spring
When she tried to hold and hold
Saying she can't leave so quick
Drawing the northern wind
She sprinkled sleet on the ground
With heavy snowflakes

A Love Letter for Unity

Gaegol Mountain, Birobong Peak
The flowers of icicles that touchingly bloomed
Have all faded away

The hoarfroast on Taebaek Mountain
The winter flowers that mysteriously bloomed
On that thousand-year-old tree have all faded away

And now, at the Halla Mountain Baengnokdam
Will bloom the nipples of red plum blossoms
Rising up from the ground

Before the plum blossoms spread its blood red
I want to see your face

Little star

Don't cry
Baby, don't cry

You're axing your tears
The sound of crying

Is poking your father
Deep in his lung
Tearing his heart apart

Don't cry
Baby, don't cry
Love hurts like that

Don't cry
Baby, don't cry
Don't cry so sadly
For you are the apple of my eye

The Herdsman and the Unfulfilled Dream

My weaver girl
Take this, too

Folded all night long
It's a ruby-colored dream

Traveling the Galaxy
Sprinkle this along

Ruby color dreams
Will bloom as star flowers

By any chance
Even if you know how I feel
Do not cry

Solitude

The snow on the branches of Milennium pine tree
Is as heavy as a burden
The morning on the ridge is still

Birds are in the sea of clouds
Their wings wet and daydreaming
The daytime sleep in a deep mountain valley is profound

The desires that once butted up the gravity feel helpless
Vain sobbing in the wind
The sea of clouds had wings in the imagination
But has lost the strength to move on

The sun that lit up the youth
Is now a fallen dusk
It casts its yellow anxieties on the mountains
Not knowing how to leave

Snow piles up on Geumgang pine tree silent for thousand years
Hangs over it the yellow anxiety of the sun
Golden snow flowers are in full bloom
The crescent moon is still on the ridge

The Spring of Flowers

Right there, in the wild grass
Inside the nest

Lark chicks
Dig out of the universe
Hitting the ground
With their sounds of crying

A sudden awakening
Of spring flower

Burning
The beautiful land of Korea

Freedom of the Soul

His life is full of dust
In the rice-bin back of the screen
There's no gold or silver treasure in it
Just full of dust

Irreducible from his life
Dust, dust, and dust

Compassion oxidized and faded of light
Torn and broken wounds
Desires that have been overturned and destroyed
People still crying and laughing
Poems that could not be reproduced as words were lost

Irreducible from his life
Dust, dust, and dust

His body and mind
The gold and silver and oxidized elements
Stuck in the rice-bin of desire
Living the punishment

Out of prison
They must return to the stars they're from
Must return to the galaxy where they used to bathe
Must take over the rice-bin ship
And they have to escape

Dreaming
The dust curls up

The Falling of Blossoms

I am a white flower
White flowers are heaven
Come find my scent

On a white windy day
Ride your white donkey
Welcome

Tap, tap, every bridge that you cross
I lie down with my white soul
My heaven is breaking grain by grain

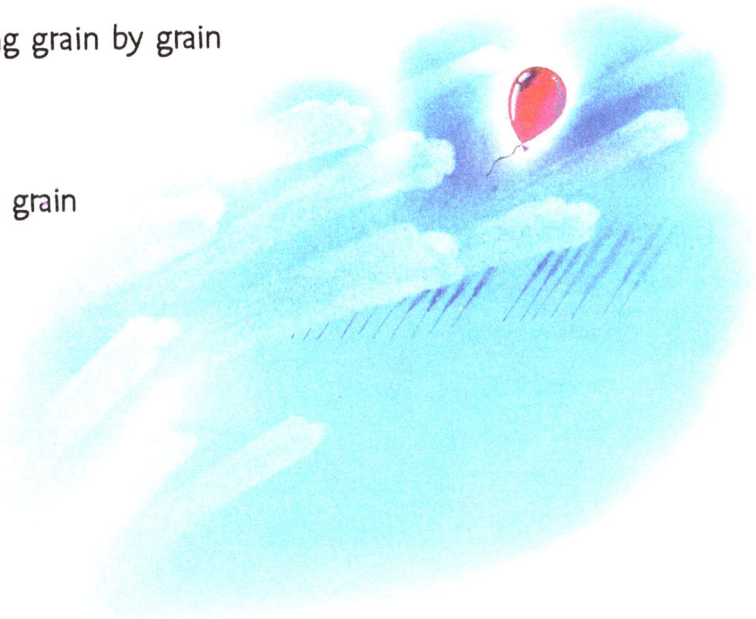

My heaven
Is breaking grain by grain

Aspiration

Life
Is yet
Early
To give up

Life
Is yet
Early
To despair

Love
Is yet
Early
To break up

As long as
The sun is blazing

PART 3

Happiness is Growth

A Slash

Love can crack
In just a moment

When it's shaking
Do not ask the wind either

When it's cold
Do not ask the Sun either

When you're lonely
Do not ask the Moonlight either

Find a blue pine tree
That has lived a life and holds wisdom
Hold onto its wide trunk and let out your tears

There you will scan the tree's heart
Read it to live your life

A person's heart can break down
In just a vain moment

A Shameful Life

Bow your head
Lower it down

Don't raise it
Or look up to the sky

The moment you raise your head
The truth flies away

The moment you show your face
Lies come to hide in there

Bow your head
Lower it down
Stick it between
Your filthy groin

That is a life of reflection

I See You

You
I see you well

Approaching from afar
I can see your smile

Trembling
I can hear your excitement

I see you
I hear you
I put the sentences into the translator of my heart

"I Love You"
"I Love you"

That is all I get
What should I do?

Please just take it
As the translator says

My face is getting red
But that's how I feel

I See You

Life

Life

Sometimes
Hurts so much. It is pain

Sometimes
Can't feel anything. It is vain

Sometimes
Pleading to death. It is love

Sometimes
Infinite feelings. It is
fantasy

Sometimes
Endless pursuit. It is
desire

In the end
Nothing. It is meaningless

An Oak Leaf

Walking along Namsan road of Seoul
The wind carries his scent
The spiral body reveals
His soft and sharp ambition

The soft and sharp ambition
The tough wind must have shredded it
And would have offset it
Presenting it to the forest family

Though afraid and scared
He would have trained himself with the weapon from his mother
To save the lives of his forest family

On the skinny, exhausted body
Between the thick and thin bones
In that database chip
He would input the traces of his life

At the home port where the spaceship is resting
Tracing back the mother-stream of the Galaxy River
The big command ship and small ships
Are orderly making their way to the star

Towards the star, towards the mother port
Going up the mother-stream
In his soft body
Powerful ambition flops

Luck

Life consists of
Seven lucks and three efforts

70% is luck
And 30% is your will

That's right
I have waited
All my life

Already
You have come and gone
And I did not know

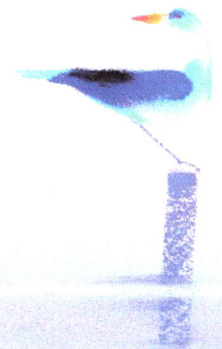

I will ask myself

At the end of my life, I will ask myself
Did you truly love the ones you love?
I will ask myself

At the end of my life, I will ask myself
Did you give warmth to your family?
I will ask myself

At the end of my life, I will ask myself
What have you done for this society?
I will ask myself

At the end of my life, I will ask myself
Did you live your life to the fullest?
I will ask myself

At the end of my life, I will ask myself
Has your life been beautiful?
I will ask myself

At the end of my life, I will ask myself
What fruits have you born?
I will ask myself

At the end of my life
To hear a honorable answer from myself
I will love the ones I love
I will obey and care for my parents
I will commit to the society by sharing and serving
I will not hurt others, and be generous
I will make joy in my life every single day
I will live a kind, beautiful life

I'm in the garden of my life
Sowing good seeds and nourishing them
I'll take care of them until they grow green
Harvesting strong fruit
Sharing with everyone
I will live my life to its full

The spring and March Snow

Lovers on a spring day
The tundra swift and grass flower
Are buried under the white roar
Unable to spread their wings
Do you know?

Do you know the pain of a swift?
A white moonlit night
In flightless footsteps
Tapping on your chest and singing
Do you know the song?

Do you know the sorrow of wild flowers?
Come into the world as a loving flower
Overpainted with your arrogant envy
They are trapped in snowflakes
Until the Sun shines on the tundra
Do you know their tears?

Invader, under your pressure
The swift and wild flower
Shed tears of blood in secret language
Do you know?

Your Confession

Your eyes are warmer
Than the sunlight

But you know what?
What's warmer than your eyes?
It's your tears
Melting my heart

In cold sleet
Even when life freezes

Your boiling eyes and tears
Melt my body down

Surrender

I hear you
Calling

The common and insignificant
Superfluous emotions

See the waves
Captured by the wind

The stepping-stone bridge
holding the hands of the stream

See how the waves and stream
And the stone bridge
Surrender to one another
Honey?

Our love
You and I
Let's surrender to our feelings

Yes, honey

The Key to Nirvana

You
To be happy
Lower your expectations for me

To gain peace
Get away from your wild dreams

You and I
Lower our expectations
Start by emptying our minds

We
Are blueprints for the future

The Flower Cup

As I smelled the flowers
I discovered the cup

As I smelled the flowers, I found
That a beautiful flower can smile
Because there is a hand
That holds up the flower with all its might

If you don't try to see it
You cannot see it
The bright flower stands out
But supporting the beauty
Are small and shabby hands

If you don't try to hear it
You cannot hear it
Faithfully supporting the flower
Are the thin sounds of breathing

As I smelled the flowers, I knew
Flowers cannot bloom
On its own will

As I smelled the flowers, I knew
Everywhere in the world, there are
Grass roots supporting the flower

Spring Sentiments

Green barley
Its blue breath
Climbs the foot of a mountain

Azalea
With a mournful look
Dreams a pink dream

The spring sunshine
Burns up the sentiment of spring

Our love
Burns hot

Unrepayable Gift, Grace

In one's lifetime
There is a gift
Unrepayable

If you received a gift
You shall pay it back
Why do you say you can't?

When your life is at stake
Or you're having a hard time
If you have been helped
Then you have received grace

Then, the indebted person
When things get better
Or he makes success
Can he return the grace
To the one who showed mercy?

It is unrepayable
All life long, it cannot be returned
The value of grace when you receive it
Is so noble that you cannot estimate it
In any material form or scale
You will not be able to repay it

I've lived my life
Receiving a lot of gifts that I cannot repay
Knowing that I cannot return it for my life
I am just a hopeless sinner

My God

He orders me to live a good life
The word of God is

Dust in the rough wilderness
And the trace of tough days

Deep in the mountains, on a dark stump
Storm pouring down

Suffered an unfortunate life
Dying in vain and disease
My friends, poets

My God
Please welcome them
Lead them into your arms

A Sealed Spring

Pressed by silence
The stuttering wave

Dazed by the bitter spring light
The lump couldn't bear to bloom, lowering its head

The whooshing whirlwind
Has lost its way

Thanks to the envy of spring, the dew in the salt field
Each of them blooms winter flowers

Every day in every step that I take
Spring eyes are about to open

Grab a handful of sunlight
And look from the shadowy color

There I meet you, the most humble
For you, my fingertips are aching with sentiment

Spring Spring Spring

You
Have no end

If
By any chance
There was an end to you

After Crossing
All those rivers

After climbing
All those mountains

Would you
In my heart
Have lit up the flower light?

Spring Never Gives Up

When the lark broods over its eggs
The Gangnam[5] swallows return with the spring

When the azalea flowers bloom,
A cuckoo spits blood, saying
It's spring and so my dear returns

When the yellow forsythia opens its eyes
The instant of spring fades
An old lady seals spring with her salty tears

Dignified beings!
Look at those living in this land

Look at them not giving up
And living intensely

Look at them in spring
Blooming brightness again
Look at the hope they have grabbed

---

5) The far southern region where the migratory bird called swallow lived before arriving in Korea.

Waiting For You on a Spring Night

The sound of blooming flowers
A horrified heart

Thinking someone might come
In search of a flower garden
I look up at the night sky

The quarter moon's belly swells up
Stars are singing in chorus with their eyes
Sending blessings

The sound of petals falling
The sinking heart
Deepening spring night
My dear, how far have you come?

Realization

Yellow cornelian cherry flowers
The dew welled up in their petals
Drip down the ground

After the tearful dew drop
Slender petals tremble

So it was
The petals tried their best
To hold on to the bright dew
That carries the sky

Who do you think you are?
Have you ever held onto someone's life?

Violently shaking yellow petals
The flowers are vigorously in love

Cornelian Cherry Flower

Tap, tap, tap
A sound comes from the blue
Are they threshing something?
Is someone's fat bursting?

A morning hung with raindrops
The sound of yellow fairies'
eyes exploding
The sound of lightening the morning
The sound of purifying the world
It's the sound that beats my heart

Fairies of soft branches
Bumping their shoulders, tap tap
Opening their eyes, the yellow fairies
The sound of their pecking
at the blue bud
Morning is tinted with yellow
Making me breathe

Happiness is Growth

Youth
Is meant to hurt

That is why
You're heartbroken
And my heart is about to break

Pain is hope
Sadness is a memory

That is why
With drooping hearts
We held hands
And had a dream

Honey
The kids are all grown up now

PART 4

Life is Strange, So I want to Live It

The Insane World

Grim Reaper
Do you make mistakes, too?
Those ugly bunch of politicians
How can you not take them?

Twice wicked than plague
That bunch of hypocrites
are causing chaos
How can you not take them?
I'm not good at anything, either
Take me with you
My fiancée trolls me every day
It's no longer worth living

Back when I was three
I went to catch fish
In that town's well
Hung pumpkin flowers
on the silk thread
But I fell plop into the water

A lady from the neighborhood came
to fetch water
She was surprised and shouted all
over town
A man passing by the old path
Came down the rope ladder and
scooped me out
Our of breath, my face blue
He rolled me up in a straw bag

The mute monk guy from the same
town
Wept, feeling sorry for me
Then, all of a sudden
I threw up, and my breath came
back
I was revived like that
They say it's a life of plus

The world shows as much as you know
And it smells as ripe as it has become
Am I undercooked?
Or am I ripe?
Am I overcooked and rotten?

Suddenly the Grim Reaper
Looks like a savior to me
And hometown seems like the underworld
I think I might be crazy
The politicians have gone insane
The world, too, is turning round and round

A Solution to Recall Memories, Wormhole

When we say good bye
To the loved ones in present life
We can meet again someday

If death tears apart
I who still live
With my lover in the underworld
Can we meet again?

From the star where we live on
My lover is setting off on a journey
To the distant Universe
How can we possibly meet?

Will I be able to meet you?
Maybe through the wormhole
Like in a science fiction movie
Summoned through the hole
Let's be a wizard

Then what shall we summon?
Shall we summon the dead?
Through a wormhole
I shall recall a memory

Let's summon my father today
To my father
I'll tell something that I couldn't say then
"Back in my chaotic puberty days
you hugged me with tears in your eyes,
Patting me on my back.
Father, I'm sorry. Thank you."

Tomorrow, I'll summon my mother
In my mother's arms
I will cry endlessly
The day after tomorrow, I'll summon my sister
I'll whine and be stubborn, saying
"Give me a ride on your back!"

From today, my wormhole
will be set on fire
It doesn't cost a penny
With no time limit at all
What a great solution!
It's a happy life

The Grass that Sprouted in the Shade Eventually Withers

I go hiking with my friends
Exploring a cave by chance
It's a shady, damp cave
I observe closely
Red bats, the king of caves,
With their sharp teeth exposed
Hang upside down and rest

The boss of the bats uses
ultrasonic waves
To set order of the cave
When an alien invader comes in,
With a raucous flight of alert
Goes into combat mode

In the cold water,
Flat, transparent, eyeless
Blind oyster-shrimp rules
Under the soil, rocks, and rotten
trees,
The millipede and the galloisiana
Have fierce competition to survive

At night, the red bats
Sneak out of the cave
Eating insects and seeds
Flying into the cave and excreting it
The guano they have discharged
Is food for cave lives
The creatures feed on it to survive

It could be the seed sprouted in the
excrement
Taking in the nourishment of the
guano
Organic and unorganic
I see a handful of well-grown shoots

It's a cave with no light
And low in oxygen
With the expectation that lack of
carbon assimilation
would hinder sustainable growth
I dug the buds out of the cave
Planted it on a sunny hill
Sprayed plenty of water

A month later, I was worried
I went to the place where the buds
were planted
The buds were all dying
Trying to save it, I arranged
some trees
Shading it so there's less sunlight
And I poured water
Now what happened?
The next time I went
They had ended up withering
and dying

Human beings have the same norm
Those who have come through
The sun, moonlight, and starlight
Stung by the rain and wind and a
severe snowstorm
Have strong tolerance
No matter how hard times are
They can surely survive
But the buds that grew in the shade
Wither away so soon
Weak people who grew up in the dark
Will end up withering away
It is the principle of the Universe

Marado Dreams of Love

The isolated Galapagos Islands
When the sun sets and darkness falls,
Marado[6] had a dream

Of ancient memories sleeping in the lake
Of the first love sleeping
in the sea, awakening
Marado had a dream

The wind paused its breath and
time stopped flowing
Stars closed their eyes
The moonlight fell on the sea and fell asleep

Putting its right arm on Dokdo[7]
of the East Sea
Its left arm on Kyongnyolbi-yoldo[8]
of the West Sea
The whale island sleeping in the dark
had a dream

Long after the Cretaceous period
when volcanoes vomited fires
When darkness fell
A porpoise swam far beyond Marado into the sea
Brought back a nurse shark and catfish
Lit up the island with a lamp

The porpoise whale crossed impossible
boundaries
Endlessly swimming to the south
Going out to the open sea
In search of love, the element that
had begun the world
It built a nest on Marado

Grandmother god woke up to the
mysterious whistling of haenyeo[9]
Hung up the lamp to light up the dark,
welcoming a baby to the world
Cut the umbilical cord of the newborn
baby, the Sun
Placed the baby into the arms
of the porpoise couple

The porpoise couple, holding the Sun
in their arms,
Isolated forever on the paradise of
Marado
Dreamed a happy dream just for the two
of them

---

6) Marado is an island situated in the south coast of Jeju, South Korea
7) A group of islets in the Korean peninsula
8) An island situated in Taean, Chungcheong province, South Korea
9) Women divers in Jeju, Korea, are acknowledged by the UNESCO intangible cultural heritage list

An Imagination Like the Lightning

Before the lightning strikes, Let's
Climb to the highest point on the ridge and catch it with a net

Will it taste hard and soft?
Will it taste like ripe mulberry at the edge of the field?

Dip the lightning in dwenjang[10]
Wrap in lettuce and give it a bite

You will get the taste
That was hidden by the Creator
What new world will it create in your mouth?

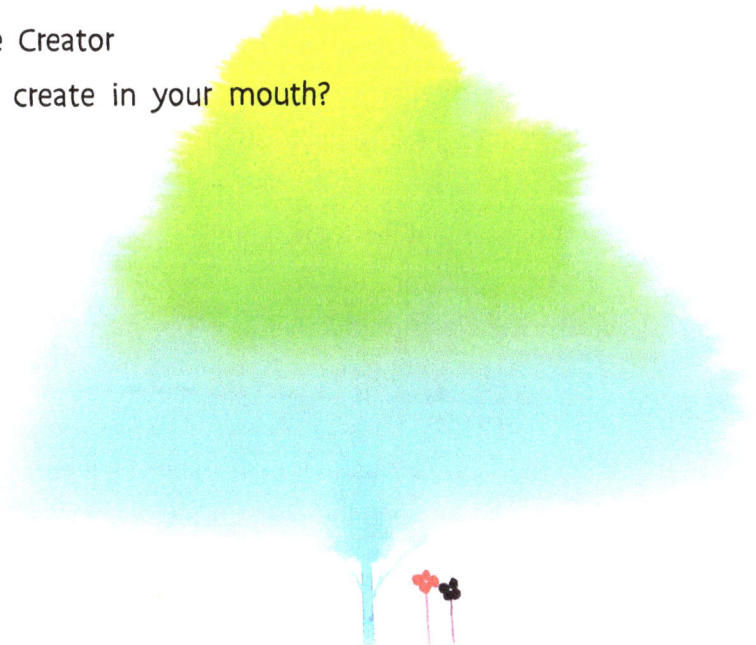

---

10) Korean traditional fermented bean paste

Jailbreak

In the muddy stream in front of Manseong-ri[11]
A pair of black walkers
Barely showing its forehead and nose
Trying to escape with a heavy breath

Born in a family, poor of poorest
Crafting bamboo combs, fans, and baskets
Less than three yards of land he farmed
Teaching and raising eight siblings
See my father's bent back

"Let me pay you back after autumn's harvest.
I've run out of money to buy the straw
for comb, fan, basket, and compost.
Please will you lend me 100,000 won?"

Ushing with the cry of the gnarled branch
Until his two feet worn out
My father tried to escape, his foot foot foot

His brother, 14 years older
Before leaving for Vietnam to join the white tiger corps
Had given those walkers, the price of his life
Worn out and flabby
My father's tenacity seeks to break out of jail

---

11) A beach in Yeosu, Jeolla Province, South Korea

Fate

You
I never taught you
Or ever rushed you
But are you moving away yourself?

Before I knew it
Your eyes
Full of tears
Are you saying good bye?

Saying sorry
And thank you
Wishing me farewell
Why are you looking back?

The Original Sin of Greed

His existence itself is a tragedy
Disaster and offender
He is called a human

Let's not do this, I cannot do this
He reflects, atones for, and prays
Yet it always misses the mark
What shall he do with the original sin of greed?

The sky is blue and clear after rain
The colorful array of seven colors
Above that rainbow
Who could put down the weight first
And reach the heaven?

Though you may try, you cannot empty it
The original sin of human only fills up
Are we captured by Arachne's rope?

A clear, dewy day
The day when the dawn is dyed with blood
A worldly man wants to abandon his greed
Sitting with a rosary, meditating and praying
He imitates the power of the gods

Moving his hips up and down
Trying to draw up psychokinesis
But nothing moves at all, perhaps the
weight is still there

To her, my pretty woman
I promised to bring a pretty star
What should I do with this?

We must cross the material boundary
Only then the original sin is cleared
That's when you can get the stars!

Fever

Falling in love with you
I was so surprised

The love that I gulped down
Got caught on the throat

Day and night
Approaching me like a creditor
You
The sound of your heart

Chanel Charm

My girl is so charming
She acts cute all the time
To me who can't buy her a fancy bag
She blooms magnolia flowers
Her cuteness points to the Chanel mark
The logo whines with her cuteness
The cuteness empties my pocket

The day I went on a trip with her,
Her charm withered
Like a magnolia closes its womb when darkness comes
The cuteness completely closed
Why, I didn't confess my love for her
I hadn't proposed her yet

I promised to build her a tree house
But her dagger flies like an angry blade
Ramming against me with pointy eyes
It's my turn to act cute
But my smile would not work out
A colt with horns on its buttocks
There is no barn to lock it up

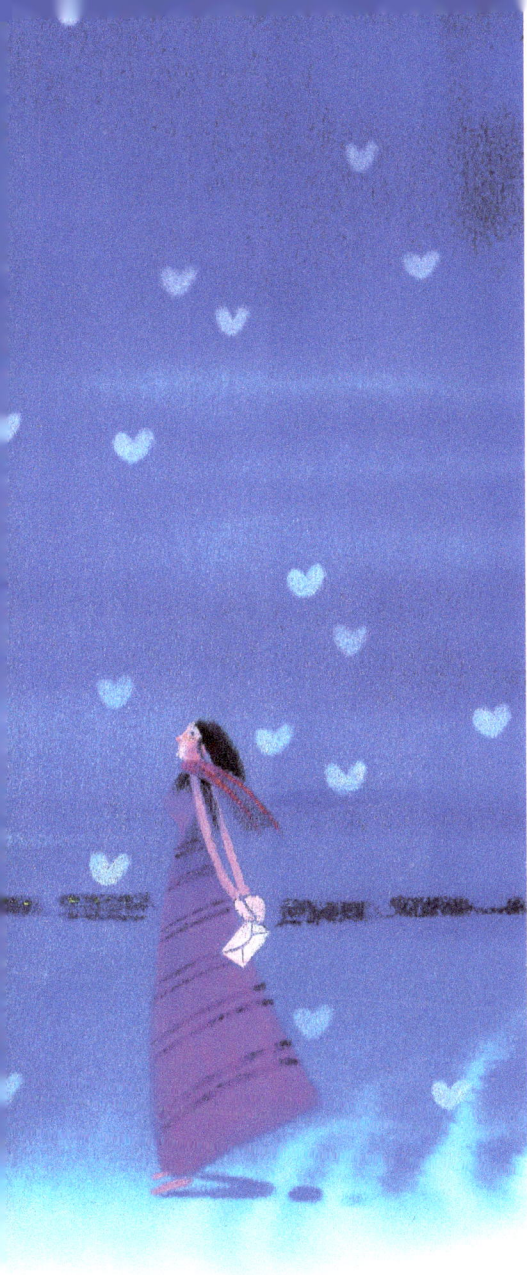

My charm cannot be a religion
Like the Lord's bell I would flatter like her slave
Being a servant worshipping her
May be the true religion
I think I'm completely entangled
My nose is surely hooked

Captured by a pretty fairy's trap
Like a fly trying to bite a tortoise
My struggle is pathetic
She's got a captive in range
She caresses the captive with her enzyme, the cuteness
It's her slave for life, her food

I lose my fighting spirit
Learning the way of life from her
Learning to obey
Polishing up my clumsy charm
I learn to put her in my heart
To put her in my eyes

A witch's law books are difficult
Harder than the bar exam
Harder than passing the civil service exam
Or even the Bible
Are magnolias stronger than poisonous weeds?
Chanel Charm is the only cure

An Iron Fortress

Do you know
What in the world
Is the
Most difficult thing?

Hmm
I'm not sure. What is it?

Picking the stars?
Winning a Nobel Prize?
Winning a gold medal?
Getting elected president?
Would it be much harder to be rich?

What
Do you think
Is the hardest in this world?

Well
To me
The hardest thing in the world
Is
Conquering your mind

A Prisoner of Love

Good-natured eyes
Are searching through the time

Struggling in an earnest trap
A grateful prisoner

Don't forget
That day, that time
The burning eyes for trust
It's blooming as a sweetbrier today

Deficiency, a Gift From God

There are many tangerine fields in Jeju Island
Orange fields in Geojedo Island

Am I right?
Lack of knowledge, lack of common sense,
Languages seem to lack a lot, too

Deficiencies are
Never so bad

Lacking knowledge, philosophy and experience
Even if you feel it's not enough
From there you urge to grow
Fiercely facing the world
Overcoming the challenges
Bearing strong fruit

The tangerine fields in Jeju Island
Are built upon
Basalts with holes in them

When rain pours on a field like this
Like water on a sponge
The basalt absorbs moisture
And slowly throws it up when he needs to
It's an automated solution

In basalt-free fields
The soil holds the water
Tangerine trees absorb as much water as they want
Ends up in quantitative growth
With much moisture
Tangerines are low in sugar

In a field full of basalt
The gravels hold water
And when the tangerine field gets dry
And tangerine tree cannot bear the thirst
The basalt minerals melt themselves
To provide their moisture
Allowing qualitative growth
Tangerines can't be sweeter

It's the same amount of sunlight
But different results
Our lives are the same

The deficiency leads us to the path of success
Showing the direction on our ways
It provides data
It is a solution

Deficiency drives desires
So we desperately overcome it
Fiercely challenging to reach the top
It is the source of
Making us grow and mature

In the course of life, our deficiencies
Could be a blessing from God

A Miracle of Happiness

"Excuse me!
Dwenjang soup is cold. Can you please heat it up?"

"Oh, really? I see!
I'm sorry.
Let's warm it up again."

"Excuse me!
We're out of side dishes.
Please can you refill them?"

"Oh, really? I see!
I'm sorry.
I'll bring you more."

"Excuse me!
The food doesn't taste good.
I can't eat it because it's too bland."

"Oh, I see! You're right.
You could add salt, salted shrimp, or seasoned red-pepper sauce.
Mix it well and try it again.
The taste will come alive.
I hope you have a happy meal time."

The customer who came alone is very picky
But the owner smiles
And gives his best service
What's amazing is
The word of a happy owner
"Oh, really? I see."
"You're right"

It's peaceful again inside the restaurant
Everyone is happy again
Maybe the owner is just being kind
Just for his business

But when he says, "Oh, really? I see!"
"You're right."

It is based on the precondition
That from another person's perspective
It could be different

When someone makes me angry
Take a breath instead of a fight
Try to calm yourself down
With a gentle smile
Let's create a happy miracle

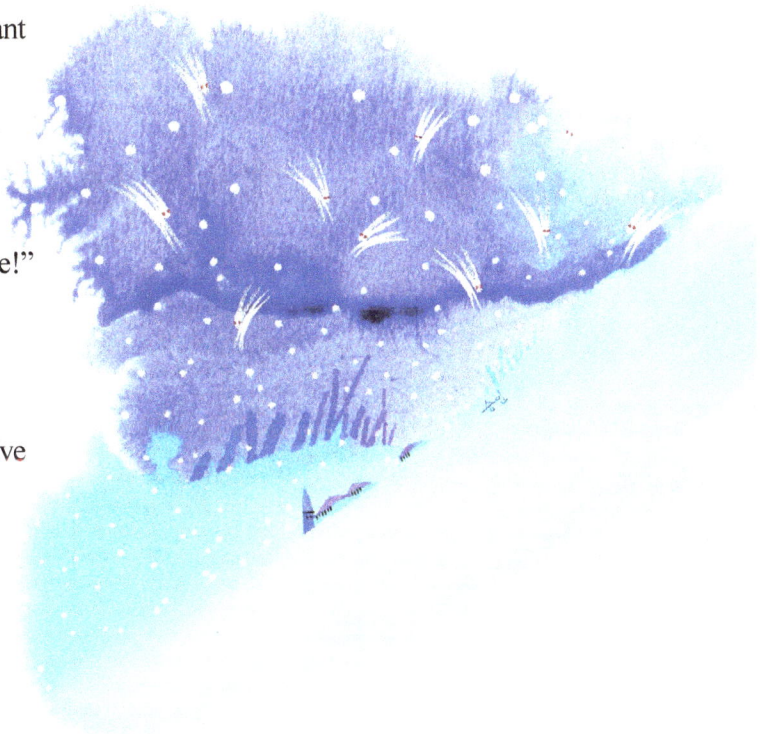

Cheer Up

You
Suffering your life

You
Since you came into the world

You
Are the main protagonist

Your existence
Is as gigantic as the ocean

Just
A little more
Cheer up

It's Unfair, But Hang in There

What's more important than talent?
It's boldness and persistence

People's memories and reminiscence
Are very inaccurate

It's the same as your company
It barely has memory

I know it's unfair
But hang in there
Fiercely, hold on

Life is
Holding on with boldness
And beating with persistence

Self-teller

In different circumstances
I talk to myself

"What's this?
It's not good.
Okay, good job."

The words that we hear from
Our parents and people around
Are imprinted, embedded, and reflected

Then we grow up
And face similar situations
The one inside ourselves
Teaches us how to talk
And gives us hints

When I have to make actions
Or react to things

I can do it.
I can't do anything.
Yeah, let's do it.
Cheer up!
Good.

These reactions are reflective
In any conversation with another
person
It's revealed in any relationship

I'm full of regrets
To the children, to that person
I said it in a negative way
I spoke in command
I shouted, too

The pain I got in the past
You must have been hurt as well!

I'm sorry. I'm so sorry

Between parents who always fight
How anxious you must have been!

To myself And to all the
other people
I have to change
And I must change

An authoritative tone
The angry tone
I was pointed out by him, too
I thought he was looking down on me
Emotions spilled out

I could have been grumpy
But I pressed down my heart
That's right.
I admitted it

I was going to organize my thoughts
Before I say it aloud

Yes, this is the new beginning
Step by step, let's walk towards happiness
Okay, let's put this into action
I can't wait to see how I will change in 10 years

A Feeling of Waiting

At the spot where I promised to meet you
While I wait in silence
A sharp knife-like kill heel sticks in

The sound of delivery motorcycles
Or politicians arguing in a square frame
All those boring language games
Penetrate me as stress

Waiting is
A heart-wrenching
Heartbreaking thing
Anyone who has waited knows

Is it you with long hair?
Maybe it's you
The expectation that you'll be next
All the closing door sounds penetrate me

After a long, long journey
I'll come to you
You walk a thousand miles out of breath
My snoring cylinder waiting for you
Raising my blood pressure, walking in seven-league boots
I run to you

Wound

I heard
Someone say

It's not a smart person
But a lame one
Who stays at one company

What?
Look at me
I've been working here forever

Are you saying
I'm incompetent?

Are you saying
I have to
work
or quit?

Seriously
What do you want from
me?

The Law of Echoes

People who enjoy their lives
know the law of echoes
The echoes sound the same
They come back to us

If you scream at a mountain or valley
The same sound comes back
If you curse, you get cursed
If you bless, you get blessed
It all comes back to you

People who enjoy life don't complain
They do not talk behind someone's back
They never turn people against each other
Because they know the law of echoes

Even if I curse, the person may choose to refuse it
He knows the curse comes back to him

If he absorbs it
It can be a blow and a shock
But if they don't absorb it, it will return to me
He knows that it will hurt himself

I'm Trying to Live

Life is
Full of tragedies

The more
You think about it

The longer
You live through it

Tragedies
Come endlessly

Even so
If you decide to live
If you make up your mind
To live somehow

Life is also
quite a comedy

Life is Strange, So I Want To Live It

Yesterday
I went to a reunion

Gildong was there
Malsook, Gilnyeo, and Geon were there
Anyway, a lot of people came

And guess what?
My eyeballs flipped over!
My friends back in school
Weren't really smart
They were of little importance

But look at them on Mercedes-Benz
On BMW
With a driver

Carrying a Gucci bag
Wearing a mink coat
The dwenjang[12) girls

Maybe I should change
The school education

Life is
Not in the order of grades
Even if you come last
Even if you don't study
You can still succeed

---

12) A slang that refers to women who chase luxury brands

A Strange Logic To Be Beaten To Death

I mean you.
You've been wrong

In the end
The very end
What's left is
Not your spouse

It's your kids
And just a photo

The Rank of Poets

When I was a rookie
I hit the sky

Hiring the speaker as a part-timer
I hid the content in a wrapper
And delivered it by quick service

Reading the theories and folk-tales of
The decendents of Hunminjeongeum[13]
Seeing the vowels and consonants,
I would scribble
With the force of a strong wind
I tapped on the keyboard

I created a poetic language a
nd registered it
on Haerye[14] Allowing slangs
and coinages
I thought I was such a valuable stone
So superior
I thought I was flawless

After a long time, I looked closely
at the Haerye
Every single stanza and line
was embarrassing
Each poem was a pathetic one

I could not bring disgrace
On the blood of Hunminjeongeum,
theories and folk-tales
So I set a paper grinder
On a late-night snack table

I would write in Spring, and feel
embarrassed
in Summer
I would write in Summer, and feel
ashamed in Fall
I would write in Fall, and feel miserable
in Winter
So it will be the same next season
I want to break the brush and smash
the table

For this very reason,
The Chinese poet Gojeok and
Goryeo[15] poet Lee Gyu-bo
Would have wasted time fishing poems
with drinks and harps
And when they finally aged
Reached the rank of poets

---

13) The early version of script of the Korean language, Hangul
14) The footnotes of Hunminjeongeum
15) One of the states founded in 918 during the Korean Three-Kingdoms period

A Superb View of the Yeongsangang River

Chuwolsan Mountain[16], where birds sing clearly
At Damyang Lake, where the Yeongsangang River starts
The light of the mountain pours down, turning the water crimson red
Walking in dugout canoes, tiny like flower shoes

In the late spring, along the furrows of the field
A mournful string of Arirang
The Sigimsae Melody[17] fills the lake
Chuwolsan Mountain glows with sunset
The late mountain pitch blossoms are ripening red

In the dusk
The moonlight is finer than the flesh of a mountain lady
Ganggangsullae[18] with starlight along the Yeongsangang River
Hoping that the path of a traveler won't be too long
The scops owl sorrowfully cries

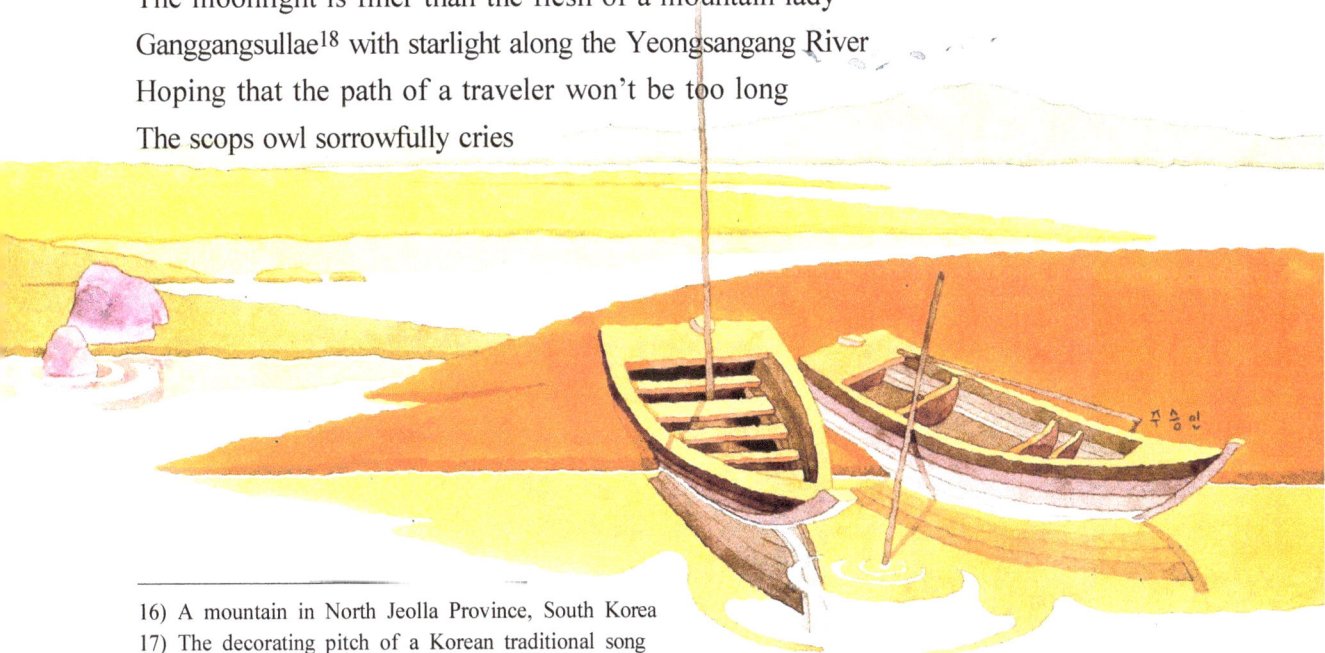

16) A mountain in North Jeolla Province, South Korea
17) The decorating pitch of a Korean traditional song
18) Korean traditional ritual that involves dancing around in circles, holding hands

Flower

She who will devote herself to the deceased
Blooming her buds in a flower garden
Their springs splashing with one another
Full of passers-by

There is fragrant honey in her well
Endlessly springing up
For her fragrance and affection are so deep
The travelers who ran from door to door
Fold theirs wings and stick them down

Folding her sharp tentacles
Permitting her womb where honey flows
Letting the muddy, dirty smells rest within her scent
She throws herself into the flower path
Creating the world I shall complete

Love that I can only achieve by throwing myself
Love that I can only achieve by bearing pain
Whose spring of flower could I be?
Whose flower path could I be?
Could I give off a scent on my own?

Travelers make a fuss at night in front of the branch doors
When star flowers bloom and dew falls to earth
She locks up her womb
Mourning at the funeral of the Sun

PART 5

A Swing For Two

A Large Island of Water

In the middle of the West Sea
Soyado, a small but beautiful island lives
Right next to it is the mother island,
Deokjeokdo
Holding the legend of a big water island
The wash painting of Seopori beach
Is the figure of an infant
Held in its mother's arms, drinking milk
A dreamy nest, fairy-tale land, and paradise
On the gravel beach, coming as a bonus
The pebbles dreaming dreams
It's a healing beach of rolling romance
Close your eyes and taste the sound

The black-tailed seagulls nesting
on the island's cliff
Ovulate and lay eggs
The cormorant swallows up a mouthful
of food
Feeding the chick and drying its wings
Sail out to sea for two hours or so
There's an endless hours of scene
Of dolphins swimming by
These legendary stories
Come delivered right in front of your eyes

Clams, oysters, seaweed, seaweed,
flatfish, flounder,
Rockfish, croaker, wrasse, conger eel,
conch, octopus,
Abundant fish species such as octopus
and stone crab
And many reed reservoirs on the island
are playgrounds for freshwater fish
Sea snail, mudfish, turtle, freshwater
shrimp, crucian carp, and freshwater eel
In the mountains are roots, shiitake,
grapes, bracken,
Chestnut, Dalrae, mugwort, horseradish,
dandelion…
Dozens of species of herbs and fruits
reside
Specialties like black goat, arrowroot
syrup, salted clams
Without hesitation, rub cheek-to-cheek
with tourists and fishermen

By the time I'm on my way around
I see rocks of abundant stories by the seashore
The long-time stories of fishermen and avec
Under the foot of a tour around the island
The deep blue world is full of excitement
The juicy meat that flows in the water
Is food for the wind

Pushed by the wind that's full
I climb the Guksubong hill
Just like an ascetic reaching the stage
of nirvana
Climbing up the rock of phallus
The wind blowing into my groin
The thrill is solely because
At the breast of the sea,
the mother of mothers,
Conquering and indulging her nipples
Feeling frightened while
My naughty instinct insults the temple

The lighthouse is always a widower
But never lonely
The sea, with its white affection
Often says hello

The fisherman grunts and lifts the boat
Love comes and farewell goes
Black-tailed gulls and cormorants
Are extras carrying excitement

Hear the serenade of the Moon and stars
Feel my tears well up
I fall asleep to the sound of a lullaby

The big water island hugged tightly by
the mother sea
Becomes a mother before I notice it
We cuddle into her arms
An apple doesn't fall far from the tree
Her motherly love, the mother's flower,
and mother's tongue
Purify our eyes, ears, and images
We feel lucky
Everyone is happy
We lie on our backs
Humming
Becoming each other's lighthouse

An Archeopteryx

Is it a bird?
Or a reptile?
Could it be a mammal?
Shriek! Caw, caw, caw!
It soars up in the sky

A dinosaur book might say
It is a monster
Or a revolutionist
Blending into the reality and future
Adapting and evolving
A creature of dominant genes

Shriek! Caw, caw, caw!
It flies through the primordial sunlight

Back in Jurassic period
It gained its name, fossil
Rumor is that
It is a poet, essayist
Or a novelist

In the mainstream of Jurassic Tribal Society
Are the carnivorous Tyrannosaurus
Envied him
Flying freely in the sky

They, too, wished to fly
Wildly shaking their four legs and tails
But not even an inch they could fly
Their stomach burped
The bodies got stuck in the mud
Methane gas released from their belly
Contaminated the society

In the dinosaur society
Those engaged in politics, economics, and law
Seized the hegemony
Clasping it in their hands
Hunted for money and power
To seize even the power of the sky
Tried to surpass their talents

While they lacked nothing
Their desires went beyond the limits
Crossing the critical point between heaven and earth
Transcended the power of God

Shriek! Caw, caw, caw!
Shriek, shriek! Caw, caw, caw!
The fossil evolves and resurrects in the 22nd Century
Scolding the humanity

Nokdu's[19] diary

- Black rubber shoes

Early in the morning, my mother
Would place purified water on the refining stove
Say a prayer
Father would polish the black rubber shoes
on the stone
For me and my younger siblings
who would wear them to school
We would pack our bags in cloths
To put over our shoulders while we run
Nuna[20] would pack yellow lunchbox
For us little boys

Eat barley rice for breakfast with kimchi
on the side
Run ten miles with a bundle of books
on our shoulders
When we reach school, our stomachs feel hollow
We're hungry and starving

Adults call it the Barley Hump
They tell us not to run
Or we'll get hungry again
The long-awaited lunchtime is back
I opened my lunchbox
Barley rice with kimchi and anchovy on the side
Mixed well on the way, I stuff them in my mouth
In that ten miles of run, they would have
bumped into each other and mixed in one place

I asked my teacher in science class
"Physical forces work behind your back
An the law of inertia worked.
It's called automation."

HB pencil doesn't write well
I dipped it on my tongue and wrote.
On a test day, the fellow sitting right behind
kept poking my back with his pencil
to hand over the cheating sheet
It hurt so much that an "ahh" sound came
out
Got caught by the teacher and he took away
the test papers
Had to hold my chair up high and get the
punishment
I did a week of cleaning the bathroom

On the way home after school
Bathed in the stream
Feeling hungry, I gulped down the stream.
The belly gets plump like a pig's belly
Jiggling
My head starts spinning
I see a white moon ghost

---

19) Nokdu, meaning mung beans, used to be a common name in Korea
20) Older sister

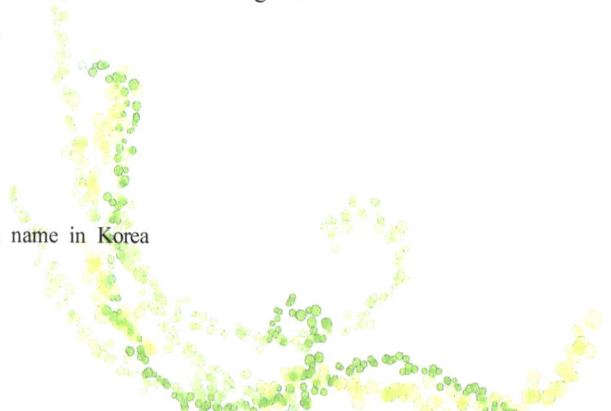

My younger brother and I picked marsh snails and clams
Filled two pairs of black rubber shoes with them
Bundle of books slung over our shoulder
Holding the pairs of black rubber shoes in each hand
Brought it home safe as if we're holding gods
in our hands
Mom washes the snails and clams
And adds dwenjang
I put the pot on fire
A few days ago, I'd been to a distant mountain
with Mom
When I throw in the pine branches we'd collected
The spicy smoke climb high into the sky and does
a shaman dance

Mother and sister
Scooping out snails and clams
Adding mallow to the dwenjang soup
Putting various seasonings and boiling the soup
A pot full of bean sprouts and barley rice
The whole family gathered for dinner

It's all thanks to the black rubber shoes
I have rubber shoes, so I go to school
Gather clovers
Play hide and seek
Run errands for Mom and Dad
Catch and bring in marsh snails and clams

If I can, from tomorrow
I should take off the black rubber shoes so
they won't wear out
I'll carry them in my chest and walk
Serve them sincerely like my god
Because it's my number 1 treasure

(End of Nokdu's Diary)

For dessert, I feast on the snails and clams
Took off the tail of the marsh snail with my front teeth and sucked
Bitter meat and juice
Popped in my mouth, really tasty
My brother was greedy and tried to eat a lot
His front tooth snapped

The naughty boy starts crying
Still, I won't cry
And finish the rest of it

New world

"Come out, Avinus.
Guide me to Prince Jiyul
Of the legendary bamboo kingdom."

"Here I am, Colonel Avinus.
Master, you're still as beautiful as
dawn I saw at the beginning of the world.
But why might it be so that
You're looking for the prince of bamboo kingdom?"

"Yes, that prince holds the power of utopia
That I forever dreamed of.
He writes poems of eternity
And has eternal love.
I want to accept him as my husband."

"Yes, my majesty.
I will follow the orders of Princess Biju of Joseon.
Please, get on my spaceship."

The spacecraft crossed the Ural Mountains
Passing through the Altai Mountains,
Arrived at the mysterious bamboo kingdom
Hidden in the rugged mountains of Baekdu

Approaching the secret of the bamboo kingdom
The princess stands at the crossroads of a new destiny
This is a paradise where
You cannot find confusion or passion of human beings
Away from the winds and waves of the world
Even aging and death pass by

This bamboo kingdom is surrounded by rugged mountain ranges
Mysterious land completely cut off from the outside world
Once you set foot here
Until the prince approves
It's hard to escape
Time passes slowly
And the water of immortality flows

You could live up to several hundreds of years
Healthy as your 30s
A peaceful kingdom freed from the worries and pains of everyday life

The utopia the princess had dreamed of
She finally meets Prince Jiyul
Living in this peaceful world
Avinus guides her to the prince

"It's an honor to meet the legendary Prince Jiyul.
I brought to you my master,
Princess Biju of Joseon."

"I am Princess Biju of Joseon.
I'm pleased to meet Prince Jiyul, who is my ideal.
I have been deeply in love with you for a long time.
I want to marry the legendary Prince Jiyul.
If you don't allow me,
I am going to die here."

"Princess Biju,
this is a land of immortality.
I want to die, but I can't.
I want to grow old, but I can't.
And I am already a thousand and two hundred years old.
Are you sure you want to marry this old man?"

"Yes, my prince.
You're the legendary hero
And my master.
If you accept me,
I will love you and serve you for eternity."

"Princess, but to me it's a shame
That I cannot grow old or die.
I want to return to your land, Joseon,
And live a happy life with you.
That is my dream.
Would you do me the favor?"
It's my wish, will you grant it?"

"Come out, Avinus.
Put the ship on hold.
Let's go to Joseon with Prince Jiyul.
Serve the prince."

"Yes, my majesty.
I will serve the two of you.
Please, get on the spaceship.
I will bring you both to our home."

What would happen to Princess Biju and Prince Jiyul
After they had returned to Joseon on their ship?
Would they marry and live happily ever after?
Would they live forever, neither grow old nor die?
Or would they meet the end of their fate?

The new world that humans endlessly pursue
Does it really exist?
Alexander was endlessly searching for a new world
All over the world he traveled and conquered countless countries
But in the end he could not find the new world
He died away from home
And the land he conquered, the Macedonian empire, successor of Rome,
Also came to a fall

All beings dream of a fairyland
Where years pass slowly
Where the water of immortality flows
An indestructible utopia
We endlessly dream

In the distant future, when science develops further
And medicine more advanced
As intelligence and character develop,
Could we build a utopia on this land
Where our ideal comes true?

Imagination belongs to everyone

Eureong[21] Swing

The waves
Come and go
Swept away and return

The tree
Dressed in spring
Take off clothes in winter

Circular and obedient
On the road of reincarnation

You and I
Are connected

Spring day
The most beautiful moment in our lives
Is it real, or just a dream?
Flowers bloom and wither,
bloom and wither

You wither
And I wither, too
We know that obvious bud
But why did we bloom it again?

But if we hadn't bloomed
There would be no love

Swaying in the wind
The path of pain that blooms and
withers

Still, if we hadn't walked the path
We wouldn't have laughed and cried

You and me
Climb the Eoureong Swing
Dudungsil[22], dance together

Whoi![23]
Ulssu![24]

---

21) Means a swing for two
22) Filler words in Korean traditional dance
23) Same as above
24) Same as above

Snow Liverleaf of Yongheungsa Temple

The spring snow is still here
Spring wind adjusts my clothes, and sunlight cannot open the side door
Creeping through the cracks of the door

A girl pulling a string of sunshine
Pushing up the remaining snow with her soft, downy ears
Soon to open the flower palace
Her affection spread out in places
Love tempts the clumsy spring wind

A longing buried in the snowflakes
One spring light walking in flower shoes
Into the sweet smell of milk
The girl tempts my heart
Spring blooms with love

The Love between Falling Water and Stone

From the eaves of a thatched house
Falling water

Tip
Tap, tap
Tippity-tap
Tippity-tapp a-tap
Tap, tap, tap

Water droplets falling on the stone
When the sound of 'plink' explodes
A rainbow blooms

Two 'plink, plink' drops of water
A double rainbow blooms

Falling water caresses the stone
The delicate love of fine water droplets
A thousand times, ten thousand, millions,
and
tens of millions of times
When poured, miracles happen

A small drop of water
The falling water that was said to be
weak
Ten years, hundred years, thousand
years of hard work
Rings the heart of the stone that was
so still and quiet

The sky seems to help the water
It's the balance[25] of Yin and Yang
Falling water has courted the stone
For all his life
That stone allowed her deep heart

What great love

---

25) The balance of negative and positive in oriental cultures

A New Year For a Tree

New shoots sprout and leaves grow
Blooming buds and spreading wings
Believed that the world would flow with the
scent of honey

A sunny day
The flowers are in full bloom
and the wind blows
The day the lark blows the grass flute
Bees and butterflies with intense love
She believed she would
bear abundant children

But in late spring the well dried up
In summer, she lost a child to a typhoon
She also broke her shoulder and back
In winter, the uninvited guest from Siberia
Took away her clothes

But don't worry
Hot blood flows through my body
My roots pump the water of life from
the earth
Every joint of my shoulder will conceive
a child
Tucking them into a good night's sleep
Waiting for the spring

Do not see my naked body
And shed your tears
I lived hard all year long
It was rewarding and happy

Even if the new year brings pain again
I will put up a new shoot
Growing leaves and sprouting buds
Producing honey scent
And bear beautiful children

A Thief's Original Sin

"Honey, can I steal your heart?"
"What will you use it for?"
"I'll hang it in my heart."
"Yes, you can steal it all.
I'll leave the door wide open
Shall I give you the key?"

The most beautiful thief in the world
I used to be a thief, too
I stole the heart of this dainty and pretty thief

On this star we live in
If only these thieves wandered around
The world would become bright, fragrant, and worth living in
But it's full of thieves who steal other people's properties
The world seems doomed

"Baby, you can steal away my heart.
Clean it well, polish it, and carry it in your arms for life.
I could live as a servant in your heart.
Don't throw it away just because you're tired of it. Bear me forever.
I will ring the bell until the day
I pay off my debt of stealing your heart."

Hometown

The legend that I miss

Dancing cosmos swish
and swoosh
Dying the blue sky

Dragonfly chasing round
and round
Autumn ripens red

With longing, and with yearning
Playing hide and seek
every night
Following the traces in
my dreams

My hometown, faint in
my dream
Is the house of white lotus and
bamboo wine

Rice bowl

Mankind discovered fire
Cooking and eating, he was born
Handling fire, developing cooking
The history of mankind has developed
by tasting the taste
Thanks to the nourishment of food

Even while skipping meals, still
energetic enough
Children grow up in winter
The back of their hands burst
and ears tingle
But rolling the snow and sledding
They play with icicles and measure
their height

During the farming season when adults
take a break
Children cannot stand
To the windy hill, to the field
They run away to the river
Eating rice cakes or sweet potatoes that
the mothers steam
They runs and frolic, ignoring the cold
But in that winter their bones ripen
The power of the rice bowl, the power of rice

Every morning we worry about our meals
If there is no smoke in the chimney
That house is starving today

Starving, getting sick and dying out
Parents would delay for two or three
years
To put their child on their family
register

Those days of poverty
How earnestly they wished for blessings
That the clothes, pockets, bedding, braids,
spoons
Were all decorated with the word
'blessing?'
A young child was sent to a wealthy
family
Working and cooking in return for food

The power of rice is absolute
According to age, according to the
workforce
The rice bowl also changes to a larger
one
Workers ate from big bowls
It was barley or multigrain rice
Quickly digested, always feeling hungry
If you did not work,
You could not feed yourself or your
family
Rice bowl is the history of this land
When rice meant labor force

Sharing and Volunteering, A Precious Value

While peeling peanuts
I came to an understanding
When one of the two nuts in the shell
Is relatively large
The other is always small

When one grows bigger in a peanut shell
The other must become smaller
This balance
Isn't it the most basic principle in our life?
Isn't this the truth?

If I grow too big, the other gets small
The smaller I become,
The bigger others grow
That means the other person is
as precious as I am

A society where you and I can be one
With balance and order, there will be no
conflict
It is possible only when we value each
other's company
And keep the mind of coexistence

We have neighbors who sacrifice and
overcome their pains
Some are poorer and going through
difficulties
With the spirit and practice of sharing
and volunteering
We should open the life
Of hope and gratitude

Life together
If you can put your mind to it
We'd become
The most blessed in the world

Dwenjang[26]

He is the virtuoso of single-mindedness
Even mixed with other foods
He is a species that never loses his taste

He is the virtuoso of perseverance
He does not change through the years
But gives a deeper taste

He is the virtuoso of mindlessness
He quietly breaks down fat
That causes countless diseases

He is the virtuoso of kind-heartedness
He lessens the spicy taste
And softens the bitter taste

He is the virtuoso of harmony
Goes well with any food
Creating harmony with other species

Today's dinner
Is going to be a feast with
The saint of all virtues

---

26) Korean traditional soybean paste

Tteokguk[27]

Made a few days ago
The hardened rice cake
Bake it on a brass grill
Cook until golden brown

Dip it in grain syrup
As the sweet and savory taste fills your mouth
Another year is added to our age

My older sister cuts rice cakes on the wooden floor
Broth boiled in mother's cauldron
Add sliced rice cake and boil well

When dawn breaks
Set it on a charye[28] table
Let our ancestors come and eat first

Family sitting down to eat
The sacred feast of charye
Flowers bloom on the ancestors' faces
As happiness blooms in the hot rice cake soup

27) Korean traditional soup made of rice cakes
28) Ancestral rite

Father and the Spirit of the Chambit

- The Breath of a Soul

Tonight, the full moon embraces an exceptionally large jar
Filled with moon water, the food of my dreams and song of the ocean
Countless stars pour down in a drizzling blue color, poking through my heart
Drawing the hearts of the stars with a pastel
I tried to hold the weight of gravity
Caught by the collaboration of double nuts pressing out the urine
Thought I might become a cripple
If I got knocked out
So I ran mindlessly to the loo

That worthless fellow with no nutritional value
Let's shoot and pour it into the ashes
Feeling refreshed to have survived
Humming a song, headed back to my room
But is Father still working in his Sarangbang[29]?
The light flickering
The apricot, orchid, bamboo, and chrysanthemum
That Father had invited to his swinging door
Back in spring
Dance with black peony, master of the house

Is father busy with Chambit[30] again?
Curious, I opened the Sarangbang door
As expected, he was holding the comb
With the bright full moon by his side
Wearing a speckled bullhorn magnifying glass
Covering his knees with bull skins
Holding up the comb
Using the harmony of psychokinesis
He almost flies into the air while he concentrates on the comb

Straightening the combteeth 0.3m apart
Father's hands do a magic on the comb
A comb's spirit must come straight and alive
So that women would choose it
And it shall be loved
Its fate of being chosen to be loved
Not choosing whom to love itself
My father, knowing its fate
Grasping its spirit hard in his hands
Setting each tooth right

---

29) Korean traditional study room
30) Bamboo comb

Figures of women with an elegant charm

Black peonies dance
Plum blossoms bloom and wither
The bamboo tree decorates itself
The chrysanthemum bubbling and fainting
Father boosting his psychokinesis
Casting a spell with both hands
Presides over their enchanting harmony

Father does not notice that I'm in the room
Crossing the material world and the absolute
world
Climbing over the crown of the diagonal
lines and gaps
Marking the dot in this world and drawing a
stroke in the other world
Refining the spiritual spirit
Blowing it into the heart
Setting the comb right to straighten this
world
With the spirit of the chambit
Brushes out the corruption and decay
Filtering out the illnesses and capturing them
in glass jars
All on his own

Crossing over the authority of the gods
Whether it's gambling or provocation, he does
it all
The stars whose eyes had grown wide
After pouring down got bigger
The full moon that crossed the mountain
grew larger
Together, my dream has grown big
It's all my father's fault
It's all because of my his sorcery

'The right spirit
makes it divine and immortal'
Through his magic, Father blows in the mindset
He is a creator

Applying camellia oil morning and night
Brushing gently with the comb
The spirit of immortality, with the oil,
Smoothly
Adds fragrant color to the hair
To change the fate of the ladies
Elegant and neat with a clear scent
The grace of enchantment
It is the romance that men dream of
How could you say that
The fate of women is unhappy?
The spirit of immortality
Cannot but dwell in the women's soul

Bongchang[31] 2

It's a beautiful place
Where the light changes like magic
It's a place where a child blows a nose balloon and babbles
Through the gaps filled with hanji[32]
The sunlight that comes through the threshold is brilliant

It's a mysterious place
Holding the snow wind of apricot flowers in the hanji bed
The sound of snow flowers blooming
Faint and distant
The wind and the sea of clouds flow in through the door
A girl comes out of a hole in the fence
Meets the boy and whispers

Love love
My love

It's a place of dreams
Climbing the bamboo forest road, full
of moonlight
The sound of Father's carving Chambit
in the bamboo field
Faint and distant

The phoenix eating bamboo shoots flies away
The sound of firmiana geomungo[33)]
is deep

Where the pond calls for moonlight
Golden moon water falls like dew on
lotus leaves
When the starlight meets in the dew
Scattering galaxies
A little child's universe is mysterious

Universe, universe
My universe

---

31) Window
32) Korean traditional paper
33) Korean traditional stringed instrument

April Fool's Day

This is reporter Lee Hyun-seok of Saemmoon News special file
From the Buddha sculpture in Bulguksa Temple[34]
A jewel has been stolen
Last night when the security guard was low
The thief broke Buddha's forehead with a chisel and hammer
And took away the stone
Police has checked the CCTV cameras
And found a gang of four Japanese thieves
Lodged in a nearby hotel
They are now arrested and under investigation
For violating the law of Protection of Cultural Heritage

According to the police investigation report
When removing the jewel from the Buddha's forehead
With the impact of the pounding hammer
It is said that the Buddha's neck was cracked
By the time the Sun rose this morning
It fell off,
Making a loud 'BBUNG'
At this 'BBUNG' sound, the downtown Gyeongju
And even downtown Busan was shaken up
It's a great 'BBUNG[35]'

---

34) A Buddhist temple in Gyeongju, Korea
35) Slang for 'lie' in Korea

Damn it

A famous Kkwabaegi[36] store that appeared on TV
Near the entrance of Gwangjang Market
After waiting in two lines for an hour, finally our turn came
She and I bit into the kkwabaegi
Damn it, it's hollow inside
The bibi[37] flowers wither

She pulls my shoulder to that side, saying
Buckwheat hotteok[38] is famous, too
Sitting on a long wooden chair in front of the store
Packed four to eat and more to take home
Counting ten, all my cash was gone
Damn it, biting off the hotteok bathed in grease
The buckwheat flowers wither

Last year, on my literature trip to Damyang[39]
We stopped at a stew place
in Changpyeong market
She misses the Amppong Sundae[40]
she tasted there
Twisting her body like the Sundae intestine
She blooms her smile
Failing to find it anywhere
Ordered plain sundae for an alternative
She and I bit off the liver and lung
At the same time
Damn it, the sundae has been out for long
Mouldy flowers bloom

She babbles
It's the market at the center of Seoul city
It appeared on TV, and her expectation was
in full bloom
It's worse than Busan Gukje Market or
Jagalchi Market
She groans and groans with disappointment
Damn it, it's just like my husband
Maybe I should replace it at this chance
Groaning and grumbling
Damn it, Gwangjang Market has ruined
everything
The sun flower sets and star flowers bloom

_____

36) Twisted bread stick
37) Korean onomatopoeia for 'twisted'
38) Bread with honey and nuts inside
39) A city in Jeolla Province, Korea
40) A dish made of a pig's intestine

Money, Money, Money, Look at the Money

Your money, my money
Money, money, money

Desperate
A bloody fight
Killing and saving

What an idiot!
Out of breath
Take good care of my money!
Leaving a legacy

When you depart the world
The remaining money
How come it's yours?
It's someone else's money

He doesn't even know
That while you are alive
Money spent for a worthy cause
Is truly your money

Living a dusty life
Stupid
pitiful
Poor fellow

Geumgangsan Arirang

Verse 1

Arirang Arirang Arariyo
My love, Geumgangsan Arariyo
Crossing the crest of Birobong Peak

The bent pine tree of Birobong
Is not lonely with a rock by its side

Arari Arari Arariyo
My love, hold me in your heart

A thousand years ago, the spore flew in
A bud has sprouted in my love's heart
Summon the wind and split the rock
Bringing rain and rooting down
Feeding white snow and gaining weight
Here we have raised our love

Verse 2

Arirang Arirang Arariyo
My sister, Bongraesan Arariyo
Crossing the crest of Ongnyeobong Peak

A rock where neither grass nor flowers could live
Has been made into a paradise

Arari Arari Arariyo
Tell me the story of your first love

In a barren garden
Called for rain and the wind
Summoned the sunlight and the moonlight
With a heart of love for the sky
Peeled off the skin and ground the soul
Here now we have good, golden soil

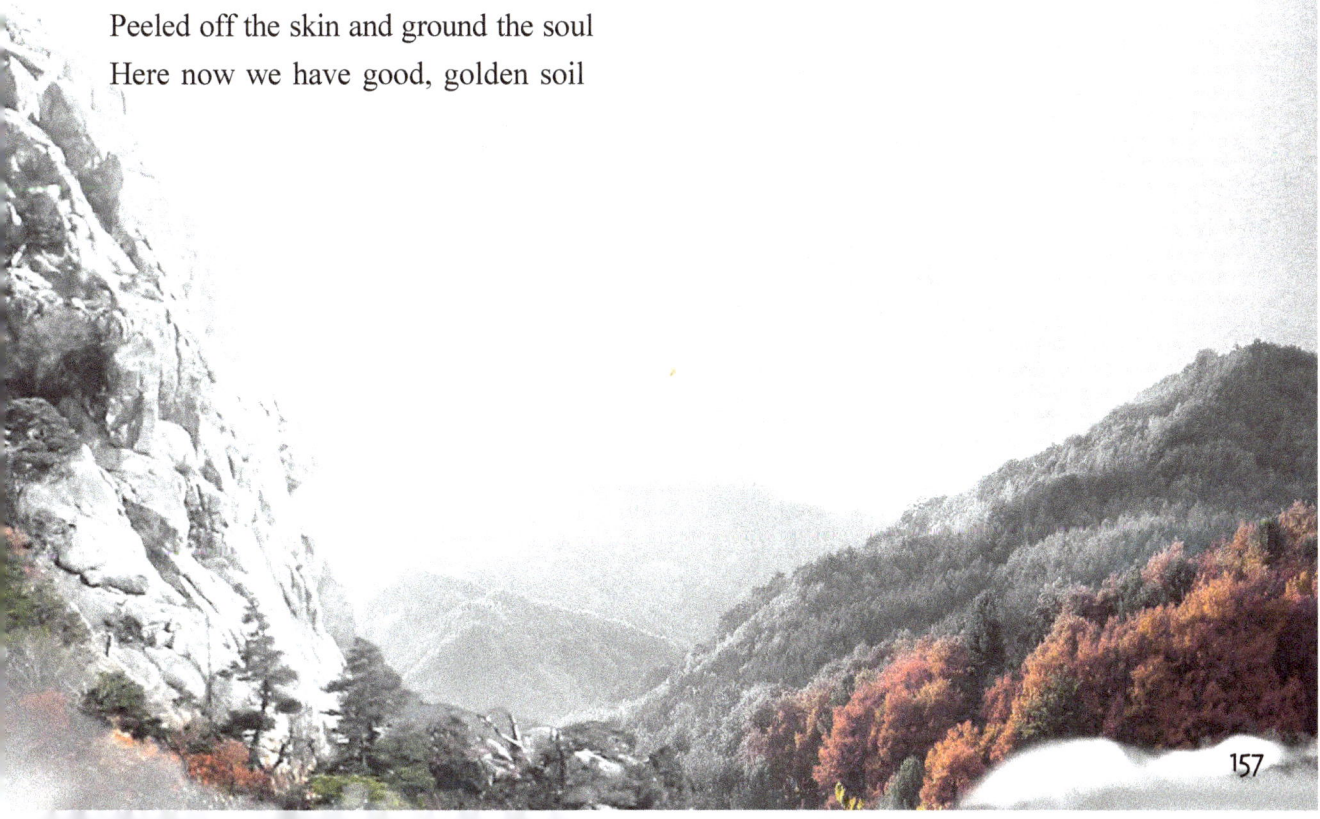

Verse 3

Arirang Arirang Arariyo
My mother, Pungaksan Arariyo
Crossing the crest of Geumsubong Peak

Fattened and given my shoulder away
Swifts and snipes sing a merry song

Arari Arari Arariyo
Mother, give me your breast's milk

Grow my bones
Widen my arms
And raised a shade
Geumgang Bellflower, Spring
Primrose, and Manlihwa
Burst their buds and shine
The world is fragrant

Verse 4

Arirang Arirang Arariyo
My father, Gaegolsan Arariyo
Crossing the crest of Wolchulbong Peak

A father's tears
Is a fountain that conceives life

Arari Arari Arariyo
Father, sprinkle your water of life

Bore and raised four children,
Naegeumgang, Wegeumgang,
Sungeumgang, Haegeumgang
And four grandchildren,
Onjeongcheon, Cheonbulcheon, and
Geumgangcheon
and Donggeumgangcheon
As for my daughter's sons,
Guryong Falls, Bibong Falls, and
Okyeong Falls
and Twelve waterfalls

Verse 5

Arirang Arirang Arariyo
My grandmother, Bukmangsan Arariyo
Crossing the crest of Geukrakbong Peak

Twelve thousand peaks meander through the sky
All who sees it will weep in tears

Arari Arari Arariyo
Grandma, take your Eollae comb[41]

To the north, Ongnyeobong, Sangdeungbong, and Geumsubong
To the west, Yeongnakbong and Yongheobong
To the south, Wolchulbong, Ilchulbong, and Baekmabong
To the east, at the Sejonbong
The maiden of the sky commands the white clouds
Holding a heavenly festival

41) A wide-tooth comb

Verse 6

Arirang Arirang Arariyo
Our Geumsugangsan, Arariyo
Crossing the crest of Ilchulbong Peak

Lake Samilpo, Lake Yeongrang, Lake Gamho
Turning crimson as she gives them a kiss

Arari Arari Arariyo
Dear swifts, sing our song for us

In spring, Geumgangsan lights a fire of flowers
In summer, Bongnaesan tints with blue
In autumn, Pungaksan burns red
In winter, the snowflakes of Gaegolsan be
in full bloom
Tundra Swifts are the heroes, protected
our Geumsugangsan
Singing The Song of the Sword

※ The Song of the Sword: Kim Hoon's novel that takes Chungmugong Yi Sun-sin as the narrator
※ Tundra: A vegetation area where tree growth is affected by low temperatures and short growing seasons

www.ingramcontent.com/pod-product-compliance
Lightning Source LLC
Chambersburg PA
CBHW081425090426
42740CB00017B/3187